Smart Serendipity

*The Essential Mindset Shift
for Time-Rich Living*

Richard Brash

For Yuko, Kaz, and Isla —
my three favourite (inter)faces!

CONTENTS

Smart /smɑː(r)t/ (adj.)

[1] intelligent, especially in difficult situations

[2] done quickly with a lot of force or effort

Serendipity /ˌserənˈdɪpəti/ (n.)

the fact of finding interesting or valuable things by chance

I've written this book to share a life of "time-rich" living.

It's not *my* life, which is why this book isn't about me. It's *your* life. Or at least it can be, and I'm going to show you how.

I call the life I'm talking about "smart serendipity."

"Smart serendipity" is that precious marriage of commitment and freedom – or "searching" and "surfing" – that helps to make our lives "time-rich."

I trust you'll find what you're looking for in these pages... or perhaps something good you *weren't* looking for will find you...!

INTRODUCTION:
HOW CAN I ENJOY TIME-RICH LIVING?

It's a common refrain: *I want more time for the things that really matter!*

Why is this seemingly simple goal of *time-rich living* so often out of our reach? We're swamped with tasks and challenges at work and at home that place constant demands on our time and energy. If we try to hurry through them we end up making compromises or mistakes, which we regret later on. So the things – often the *people* – that really matter to us end up getting our second-best. Squeezed into our down-time, they become just one more task or project. Sometimes, these things seem to overwhelm us as much as our other responsibilities.

Right across our world, statistics suggest that people are becoming ever more angry, stressed and worried.[1] A whole range of technologies are supposed to make us more time-rich, but at least the *perceived* reality is that we have less time than ever before.[2]

> → *Time-rich living* isn't just about having lots of time. That's only one side of the story. Many people do – for different reasons – have plenty of time on their hands. Perhaps they've recently been made redundant or are newly-retired. Perhaps they're experiencing "empty-nest syndrome." Maybe they are just very good at time management. *Empty* time is no good to us: it can even be torture. So the other side of the story is this: if the *time* you have isn't *rich*, you're not truly *time-rich*! In this book, *both sides of the story* will be told.

A visit to any bookshop turns up lots of ideas that offer us a new perspective. Many of these ideas are borrowed from overseas cultures. The aim is often to help us to calm down, appreciate the simple pleasures in life, and take things more slowly. Such ideas include the Danish concept of *hygge* and the Japanese *ikigai*. I really like books like these! Having lived and worked in Japan for many years, I find the Japanese concepts particularly connect with me.

But the problem with most of these ideas is that they don't often integrate well into our working lives and our relationships. Danish and Japanese people aren't necessarily more time-rich than anyone else! Japan has one of the highest suicide-rates in the world, and they had to invent a word in Japan for "death-from-overwork." Practical or conceptual hints like these books offer might help us with winding down *after* work, or making the most of the space we've got, but they don't necessarily help us get home any quicker, or enable us to finish our tasks more consistently and excellently. They might help us to put the different components of our lives into perspective, but they don't typically offer concrete guidance on the mindsets we need to bring to the challenges and opportunities that present themselves to us each day.

Of course, there are also plenty of books out there on time-management. Again, many of these are helpful, up to a point. But they tend to promote a myopic approach to life, that sees all of our time when we're not directly *focused* on something as "wasted" time. Ideas for squeezing every drop of time from the 5-minute intervals between our jobs, or our daily commute, or even our visits to the bathroom, seem to me to be not just *excessive*, but *missing the point* altogether! I think they can make the problem we feel even worse.

So, many of us remain stuck. The chances are, if you've picked up this book, you're dog-tired right now, or else you sense that you're compromising in some way: either your work, or your relationships (or perhaps both) are suffering.

A way forward: *Search* and *Surf*

The message of this book is a simple one. *It needn't be like this!*

It's possible to be *both* efficient *and* creative, time-precise *and* time-rich, task-driven *and* people-oriented, to satisfy (even exceed) expectations at work, *and* to enjoy satisfying relationships both at work and at home.

This is my experience. I'm about to turn forty. I've been working and studying for well over half my life now, often combining work and study at the same time. I've been a school teacher, a tax accountant in a City financial services firm, and a church-based student pastor, among other things. My wife and I have been married for sixteen years. We've got two great kids. I've earned various professional qualifications, two bachelor's degrees (one from Cambridge University), two master's degrees, and I'm half-way through a PhD at the University of Edinburgh. I've had articles accepted for publication in peer-reviewed academic journals, and I recently signed my first book contract. I learned to speak fluent Japanese, mostly self-taught, and in 2018 I won the prestigious Sir Peter Parker Award for spoken business Japanese at SOAS: you can enjoy the winning speech on *YouTube* if you're a connoisseur of that sort of thing. I'm also a really bad golfer.

I'm telling you a bit about my life up front, mainly so that you can see that it's been *busy*. Time has been at a premium: it still is. Also, it's not been *easy*. I've certainly had my share of ups and downs, in work and in my relationships. I've made mistakes and I do have regrets. There have been failures, for sure. Some of these stories will appear in this book. I've had to struggle with multi-tasking and demands from all sides, just like – I'm sure – most readers of this book.

But over the years I've learned a simple set of strategies and skills for coping, even *flourishing*, in the midst of a busy life. This is the secret of being *time-rich*, without losing a competitive professional edge. Friends and family have recognised these skills, and I've often been asked what the secret is. Many times, when I explain the simple strategies that I've discovered, I see a light-bulb go on, as my friend has that moment of realisation: *this makes sense!*

That's why I've written this book: to share a kind of life. It's not *my* life, which is why this book isn't about me. It's *your* life. Or at least it *can be*: of that I'm convinced.

I call the life I'm talking about "smart serendipity."

"Smart serendipity" is that precious marriage of commitment and freedom – or "searching" and "surfing" – that helps to make our daily lives satisfying and fulfilling. You could even say we're *meant* to live like this: it goes with the grain of who we are. Let me explain.

"Serendipity" means the development of events by chance in a happy way, or "the fact of finding interesting or valuable things by chance."

Sounds good, right? I mean, who doesn't want to find interesting and valuable things?

But take note! Serendipity is a *fact*, not an *act*.

Strictly speaking, you can't *do* serendipity. You can't *make it* happen. It happens *to you*.

That might be quite a humbling thought, especially if you're the sort of person who wants to take life by the horns and shake it about a bit until everything's sorted.

You can't *make* serendipity happen. But you can certainly *stop it* happening.

The word "serendipity" was coined 250 years ago, from the title of a Persian fairy tale in which the main characters – known as the "three princes of Serendip" – were always making pleasant discoveries of things they weren't looking for.

But is this the kind of life that has to be confined to fairy tales? *Not at all.*

In this book I'm going to show you how it can be one of your default mindsets, as you open yourself up to encounters with the serendipitous. If you're willing to put into practice the principles I'm going to teach you in this book, I'm confident that before long there will be another "Prince (or Princess) of Serendip" in the world: you!

At the same time, remember that this book is about "smart" serendipity. That's because most of us, at least, don't have time to wander around doing nothing particular all day, in the hope that pleasant discoveries might fall upon us. *Good things don't necessarily come to those who wait, or at least to those who wander aimlessly.*

There needs to be an element of *focus* and *discipline* to our daily lives, so that we can progress quickly, efficiently, and excellently, through the various tasks we need to do.

That's what I mean by "smart."

We're used to lots of so-called "smart" gadgets these days. Perhaps you've got a smart *phone* in your pocket, a smart *speaker* in your kitchen, or a smart *car* in your driveway? These goods are called "smart" because they (supposedly) enhance our user-experiences with their good "judgment" and (artificial) intelligence.

When I talk about "smart" serendipity, I've got something similar in mind.
But I apply the idea to people rather than to gadgets.
Being "smart" is about the intelligent use of our time and energies to get things done quickly and successfully.

You might be concerned at this point that you're not particularly "smart."
Perhaps you're starting to think this book might not be for you.
Please don't worry. I'm not referring to IQ or scores in a test.
In this book, "smartness" isn't about something we either *are* or *are not*.
Unlike serendipity, smartness in the sense I'm talking about is something we can all *do*.

If you haven't "got" it, you can learn it.

But isn't this talk of "smart serendipity" just a kind of oxymoron, a play on words, like "sweet sorrow" or "deafening silence"?
Can such smartness really co-exist with a mindset of serendipity? *Yes!*

I don't mean that you will experience this happy co-existence of smartness and serendipity all day, every day. In some ways, life has frustration built into it, and this book will not deliver you from that.

But my experiences – and the experiences of others who have received the ideas in this book and put them into practice – suggest that real progress *can* be made.

So, whether you've picked up this book *smartly* (strategically) or *serendipitously* (or even for a combination of both reasons) I'm sure you'll find plenty of interest and value here.

What this book is about: a summary

The central "technical" claim that I make in this book is that there are two different ways in which we human beings interface with the world. In more simple terms, there are two different ways of doing things, or mindsets. I call them "Form-First" (FF) and "Content First" (CF).

Roughly speaking, FF relates to the "smart" part, and CF relates to "serendipity." They're not exactly the same because serendipity is – strictly speaking – something that happens *to* you rather than something you *do*. But for now, you might want to think of them as at least closely related.

Smart: Form First
Serendipity: Content First

Every reader of this book has a natural – probably innate – preference for one or the other mindset.

To give you a basic, but concrete, idea of what I'm talking about, imagine you're standing with a bucket of wet concrete, (I told you it was a "concrete" example!) and you're about to pour it out on the floor. The concrete represents *content*. Someone operating according to an FF mindset would first put a mould on the floor, and *then* pour the concrete into the container. The container represents *form*. Someone operating according to a CF mindset, on the other hand, would first pour out all the concrete on to the floor, and *then* try to think of a way to "contain" it, or even just wait and see what shape it takes.

Here's another illustration. FF and CF are loosely related to two ways of using the internet: *Search* and *Surf*. We all know the difference between these two approaches.

On the one hand, when we open a browser window and type something specific into Google, we're *searching*. There's a focus, an element of precision, a clear objective, something *smart* about what we're doing.

On the other hand, when we click, apparently without premeditation, from one interesting web page to another, going the way that the wind of fancy takes us, and often ending up in quite unexpected places, we're *surfing*. It's usually when we *surf* the internet that we open ourselves up to the possibility of *serendipity*.

As I say, I guess we're all familiar with both these ways of using the internet.
Searching and *surfing* the internet are, in fact, just a microcosm of something much bigger: they represent two different ways of engaging with the world, or mindsets.
And, for truly *time-rich living*, we need to make good use of *both*.

I'll describe both these ways, and the preferences that lie behind them, in detail in the chapters that follow. You'll be able to see clearly which preferences are closest to your own, and probably also recognise where your friends and family members fit in.

That's the *diagnostic* part of the book, and it's in chapter 1.

Next – and this is the key positive claim I'll make – *some* of the different things we do in our workplaces, families, and daily lives, are best achieved by means of the first mindset (FF), while *other* things ideally require the second one (CF).

In other words, we all need *both* ways at different times, for the different things we do.

The **problem** (or challenge we face) is that we all, naturally, tend to gravitate towards one way of interfacing with the world rather than the other, and we're not usually geared to switching between them, or to sensing when such a switch might be useful or even essential.

Having a personal preference or orientation like this isn't necessarily a bad thing. It's natural that we have some strengths and some weaknesses. And we're all different. Experts on personality type often tell us we are either *introverted* or *extraverted*. Neither of these is "bad." Each has its advantages. But most people recognise that it's useful for all of us if we're able to operate – at least sometimes – in ways that don't come naturally to us.

Let me lay out the practical implications of what I'm saying.

There are **three basic skills** we all need to develop if we're going to get back in control of our work and our relationships, so that we can enjoy *time-rich living*: (1) a *Form-First* approach to getting things done, (2) a *Content-First* approach to getting things done, (3) the ability to discern *which* of the two approaches is required in which circumstances.

These three skills give us the rest of this book's basic structure. After the first, diagnostic, chapter, the subject of chapter 2 is how to develop the FF mindset. I cover the CF approach in detail in chapter 3. And the discernment question is treated in chapter 4. In that final chapter of the book, we'll tie all the threads together and spell out the next, practical steps towards *smart serendipity*, and the time-rich life that can be yours.

First, here's the *very good news*: I can tell you for sure that you've already got one of these skills honed to near-perfection.

It depends on your natural preference, of course, but almost certainly you instinctively operate on an FF or a CF basis, and *you're already very good at it*. You don't need to learn this skill and I don't need to teach it to you because you've *already got it in spades!* You may even be able to share your ability with someone else from the other end of the spectrum: this book can certainly help you to do that.

There are therefore just **two** basic skills we all need to develop, and one more (the one we already have) that we simply need to hone to perfection.

Just two skills? Sounds manageable, right? Here they are:

First, we need to learn how to operate in the way that is *not* our natural preference. That will probably feel awkward at first, like writing with your left hand if you're right-handed, or learning extraverted behaviours if you're naturally introverted. But it's an ability that *can* be learned.

Second, we *all* need to develop the ability to identify *which* things we do require an FF approach, and which need us to take a CF approach. This is essentially about **discernment**. It's knowing which way of interfacing is demanded by our particular circumstances at any one time, so that we don't put diesel fuel into a petrol engine, or vice-versa.

This discernment comes with experience, but the basic principles can be picked up quite easily, and I'm going to help you learn them.

So, this book will teach you how to develop these two skills, and how to perfect the skill you already have. I'm convinced they're not beyond the reach of anyone reading this page. My experience proves that there really is a way to move forward, to enjoy the *smart serendipity* that characterises *time-rich living*, to get back in control of your work and your relationships, and open yourself up to the interesting and valuable discoveries that are waiting to be found.

Does that sound good? Read on…

1 TWO TYPES OF PEOPLE

"There are some four million different kinds of animals and plants in the world.
Four million different solutions to the problems of staying alive."
· Sir David Attenborough

The natural world is fearfully and wonderfully complex and varied. This is also true of each one of the many millions of individual species on our planet. Every species has its own more-or-less unique way of solving "the problems of staying alive." Human beings are no exception. The average human brain contains a hundred billion neurons. We are complex animals, and there's a lot that we still don't understand about ourselves.

But, there are *some things* about us that are relatively simple.

Here's one of them. When it comes to our human behaviour, and particularly the way that we interface with the world, there are two types of people: *Form-Firsts* (FFs) and *Content-Firsts* (CFs).

→ "Interfacing with the world" is technical-speak in this book for the way in which we approach our tasks, goals, and relationships. In the following chapters, I'll use "interface" as both a verb and a noun. When I use it as a noun, it's because I want a general term that covers everything we do that involves something or someone else – animate or inanimate. An "interface" can be either a relationship with another person, a catch-all term for our work, or something as specific (and mundane) as drinking a cup of coffee.

In this chapter, I'm going to explain the differences between FFs and CFs. I'm also going to help you to discern which one is your natural default or preference, or where you are on the "F-C spectrum." (Not to be confused with the third-division Russian football club!) That will help you to determine your personal goals as you read through the rest of this book and begin to put the ideas into practice.

Knowing yourself

"Know yourself!" This simple-yet-profound ancient Greek aphorism was supposedly inscribed on the forecourt of the Temple of Apollo at Delphi in Greece. The philosopher Socrates taught it as the first principle of a life worth living. Centuries later, French Reformer John Calvin insisted that the sum of true wisdom is knowledge of God and knowledge of ourselves. Leaving aside knowledge of God for a moment (although I'll come back to that in the afterword to this book) *self-knowledge* must be our starting-point too.

Self-knowledge isn't always as easy to obtain as we might think. It's quite possible to convince ourselves that we're something we are not. If you don't believe me, try watching some of the contestants in the early rounds of "The X-Factor." Some of them truly believe they can sing… but they can't. Asking family and friends can be helpful, but even that isn't fool-proof. (Most X-Factor contestants bring along friends and family who tell them they're wonderful singers, only serving to confirm them in their self-ignorance.)

I've visited the ruins of the Temple of Apollo at Delphi when I was on holiday in Greece. It's a beautiful place with deep cultural significance, and lots of tourists pick up fragments of broken rock to take home as souvenirs of their visit to the "oracle." When we try to "know ourselves," it's easy to pick up fragments and fail to get to the heart of things. So how should we proceed?

There are, of course, lots of different "personality tests" that are supposed to help us with self-knowledge, usually so that we can improve ourselves, or understand and relate to others in more constructive ways. Some of these tests are quite interesting and even fun. You may have taken one or more of them. I've had to take type-indicator and personal profile analysis tests at work, as part of various team-building exercises.

The advantage of tests like these is their *complexity*. They cover lots of different factors. Perhaps you get a 4-letter categorisation that covers multiple aspects of your personality, or a graph printout showing your various tendencies. But complexity is also the big weakness of these tests.

For example, I took the same type-indicator test twice, and the result was different each time. Am I a "feeler" or a "thinker"? How can I tell? Does it really make any difference?

The personal profile analysis I took was the basis of an entire day of team training and development, but I honestly can't remember a single thing about it, except that there were lots of little graphs. The "deliverables" from such tests are just not obvious in their practical applications. At best, you end up saying: *Interesting – but now what am I supposed to do?*

The great strength of the diagnostic tool I'm introducing here is its *simplicity*. Once you know whether you are a *Form-First* or a *Content-First* type, I guarantee you won't forget it! And as you read on, the practical applications will, I hope, become very clear.

Introducing the F-C spectrum

So, let's begin the process of diagnosis. The Greek-rooted word *diagnosis* has a root meaning of "knowledge apart" or "knowledge through." It's about coming to know something by a process of discerning and distinguishing, often by means of symptoms or signs. That's what we're going to do as we think about ourselves and the F-C spectrum.

We all find ourselves somewhere along this spectrum. There will be some – probably rare – people reading this book who are more-or-less in the middle. In many "personality tests" it's a good thing if you come out looking balanced rather than extreme. After all, being less-than-empathetic is somewhere on a spectrum that leads to psychopathy!

But I should point out that it's not necessarily an advantage to be in the middle of the F-C spectrum. It may even be a disadvantage.

That's because the different situations we face usually call for a "polar" (either/or) approach. If we're looking for animals that thrive in freezing temperatures, we might visit the north pole for polar bears, or the south pole for penguins. In fact, we'll need to visit *both* if we want to encounter every polar species. But we won't find anything useful at the equator.

Being in the middle of the F-C spectrum is something we can't choose, but *remaining* in the middle is a shortcut to mediocrity. Even worse, *aiming* for the middle is sheer madness, even though some of us misguidedly try to do this from time to time. This will all become clear in a moment.

Anyway, it's more likely than not that you will have a clear and natural preference for *either* form *or* content, and this preference will shape the way you behave – at work, in your relationships and your family, and in all your daily interfaces with the world.

"Form" and "Content"

So, let's get down to business. First, some explanation of terms. What do I mean by "form" and "content"?

This theoretical section may frustrate some more impatient readers, but please bear with me for a moment.

It's important to see that *everything* we say and everything we do, *always* has both form *and* content.

It's probably easiest to visualise what I mean when you think of something you might make, like a cake, for example.

I'm not ever likely to take part in the "Great British Bake-Off" (I have that much true self-knowledge) but even I know that a typical cake contains flour, eggs, butter, and sugar. These ingredients make up the "content" of the cake. You can't have a cake without any content.

But the cake, at least in its completed state, also has a necessary "form," whether that is round or square or tiered or whatever. Flour, eggs, butter, and sugar are not "cake" until they take the *form* of a cake. The "form" of the cake might refer primarily to its final, baked, state. Or it might include the various steps involved in getting there – what we would call the "recipe."

These ideas can be applied without much of a stretch to the business world, or to pieces of academic work. For example, you might have a project that you're responsible for. Whatever it is, that project will have both form and content. Perhaps you need to compile a report for a client. The relevant information that goes into the report is the "content." The way that the report comes together, both in the process of compiling and writing it, and as a completed, polished, piece of work, is its "form."

All the above examples make immediate sense because they have a tangible "deliverable" in view, whether that's a cake, a PhD thesis, or a report for a client.

But what about other things we do? Is it really true that *everything* we do has both form and content? What about our relationships? Well, take my relationship with my son, for example. Of course, there is "content" to our relationship. The content includes such positive things as love, trust, fun, and discipline. At times, it includes negative things such as frustration and anger – on both sides, I should add! Without these things, the relationship wouldn't exist. It would be *content-less*.

But equally, our relationship takes many forms. Those forms would include all those things we like to do together, such as playing games in the park and talking at the breakfast table. It would also include all those things we don't like, but do anyway from time to time, like shouting at each other, or winding each other up.

There isn't really a "deliverable" in my relationship with my son, at least not in the sense that a cake or a report is a "deliverable." But the relationship is based on things we *do*, and so it necessarily has both form and content.

Here's a challenge: try to think of something you do that *doesn't* have both form and content. When I gave this challenge to my wife, she said: *how about* **eating** *the cake?* I'll admit that the form/content distinction has less practical relevance here, but I think it's still there.

The *content* of the act of eating is the fact of "cake entering cakehole" (as the rather vulgar British slang would have it). But even this might take many forms. *Gourmet* or *Gobbler? Fork* or *Fingers? Does my wife get half the slice?*
So I don't think she has found a true "counter-example."

In the end, I don't think it's possible.
Everything we do has both form and content.

To paraphrase the philosopher Immanuel Kant, *forms without content are useless; content without forms is meaningless.*

Everything we do has form. And everything we do has content.

The key question is: *which do we prioritise?*

Where do *I* fit in?

So, let's get back to where we started. When it comes to our human behaviour, there are two kinds of people in the world: *Form-Firsts* (FFs) and

Content-Firsts (CFs).

What exactly is the difference? How do I know which I am?

We'll start with a really simple example, which I'm sure will be familiar to most readers. Let's imagine you have to hand something in. Anything with a deadline will do.

You might think of some homework at school, or a piece of work at university or college. Or a work report, like in the example above.

Here's the question: *when do you finish it?*

Are you the kind of person who starts early, plans out a schedule, sticks to it, and finishes up with plenty time to spare?

Or do you typically leave it to the last minute, sometimes pulling an all-nighter and setting the scene for a pitched battle with the printer five minutes before it's due?

Here we have an illustration of the two kinds of people I'm talking about.
If you're the former type – the one who plans, prepares, and starts and finishes early, I'm going to wager you're a **Form-First** person by nature.

On the other hand, if you're the last-minute, get-it-done-but-only-just-by-the-skin-of-your-teeth kind of person, I'll stick my neck out and say you're a **Content-First** type.

Here's another example, to help you with your self-diagnosis.

You've agreed to meet a friend for a drink: coffee, beer, whatever you like.

When you arrange your meeting, do you like to agree a finishing-time? I mean, do you say, "Let's meet from two to three"? Or, do you usually prefer to leave things more open-ended, so that you finish when you finish, when either the beer, or the conversation, runs dry?

If you're the sort who likes to arrange the end-game in advance (even just in your own mind and not necessarily in your actual stated agreements), that's a strong hint that you're a **Form-First** type. Conversely, if your preference is to leave things more open, or you don't even *think* about a finishing time when you're setting up a meeting, it's quite likely you're a **Content-First** person.

Alright, how did you get on? If you came out FF or CF in both examples, I think we have a match! I'll explain *why* these two types of people approach interfaces like my example scenarios in these particular ways in a moment.

If you came out FF in one example, and CF in the other, don't despair – either of yourself or of this book… yet! As I said before, there are some people who are more towards the middle of the F-C spectrum. Read on, and it's likely you'll be able to make a clearer self-diagnosis before you get to the end of this chapter.

Here, I'll introduce the two "key secret perspectives" of each mindset. I call these "secret" because they are not immediately obvious, especially to those for whom the mindset is not a natural preference. They happen below the surface, sometimes subconsciously, and – like most innate habits – usually without much deliberation. Here, all will be revealed!

There are **two** key secret perspectives, because in our interfaces with the world, both *form* and *content* may be considered under two "dimensions":

(1) **time** and
(2) **space**.

In each mindset, the first key secret perspective is **time**-focused, and the second is **space**-focused.

So, I'll give you a brief, summary, explanation of the two key secret perspectives for each type or mindset. This summary will be followed some typical descriptors of each type (in contrast with its anti-type), and some examples of interfaces with which those who prefer that mindset often struggle. All of this will be explained in more detail later on in the book, so don't worry if some parts don't quite make sense for now.

The Form-First mindset

The key secret characteristics of the FF mindset are as follows:

(1) [Time dimension] **"Time is Mine"**: FFs determine how much time and energy to spend on any particular interface by the amount of time they

deem to be available to them, *not* by the supposed "value" of that interface, measured according to any other variable.

(2) [Space dimension] **"Back to Front"**: FFs interface in a primarily *back to front* direction. That is, they start with an end-game in view, and calculate from there how to engineer the interface in order to arrive at the desired result.

FFs are typically:

· Finishers rather than perfectionists.
· Realists rather than idealists.
· Conventional rather than innovative.
· Strategic rather than spontaneous.

FFs typically excel at time-management.

But they're not truly *time-rich*. Because of their tendency to prioritise *searching* over *surfing*, they often have a tough time when it comes to interfaces that demand a *content-first* approach. And so their openness to serendipity suffers accordingly: *the unfortunate truth is that they miss out on so much!*

Interfaces with which FFs often struggle include:

· Relaxing
· Open-ended social encounters
· Creative pursuits
· Open-minded, or so called "blue-sky" thinking
· Awareness and appreciation of being in "the moment"

The Content-First mindset

The key secret perspectives of the CF mindset are as follows:

(1) [Time dimension] **"My Time is Yours"**: CFs determine how much time and energy to spend on any particular interface by the "value" they attach to that interface. The value, however it is determined, is thought to be something that inheres, objectively, *in* the interface. It does not primarily depend on the situation of the CF who interfaces with it.

(2) [Space dimension] **"Front to Back"**: CFs interface in a primarily *front to back* direction. That is, they start with where they are, and move

forward incrementally, with a high level of openness to changing direction or even finishing without a resolution of any sort, if circumstances demand that.

CFs are typically:

· Perfectionists rather than finishers.
· Idealists rather than realists.
· Innovative rather than conventional.
· Spontaneous rather than strategic.

CFs typically find themselves encountering richness at every level of their lives.

But they're not truly *time-rich*. Because of their tendency to prioritise *surfing* over *searching*, they often have a tough time when it comes to interfaces that demand a *form-first* approach. And so their lives are characterised by a lack of smartness: *the unfortunate truth is that they fail to make good on so much promise!*

Interfaces with which CFs often struggle include:

· Decision-making
· Hard conversations
· Deadlines
· Sealing a deal
· Turning dreams into reality

Well, what do you think? I guess most readers will be able to see themselves as closely associated with one or other of these mindset-types. Remember that we're talking about your *natural preference*, here. I've no doubt that some people reading this book will already have made strides forward in operating according to both mindsets – but I'm pretty sure you'll have a closer natural affinity with one or the other.

Remember that *the main thing I want to help you with* is to develop the mindset that is *not* your natural preference. But at the same time, it's no bad thing if you can work on your natural strengths too.

So, you have a choice about how you read the next two chapters. I've written them so that you can read them in either order. You can start with your natural *strength* or your natural *weakness*, it's up to you![3]

2 THE FORM-FIRST MINDSET

"Hard work increases the probability of serendipity."
· Ken Poirot

"One thing I've found... the road rarely rises up to meet you until you've begun walking."
· Michele Jennae

This chapter is all about the *Form-First* (FF) mindset.

I'll explain in detail what it is, how it works, and how to develop it, using real-life examples and comparisons so that you can clearly see what I'm talking about.

Remember, FF is one of the two basic mindsets that we all need to learn, in order to enjoy *time-rich living*.

The FF mindset is the path to the "smartness" part of *smart serendipity*.

In chapter 1, we saw that there are two types of people in the world.
Some readers will naturally default to an FF mindset. That's their type.
If that's you, you'll find much in this chapter that makes immediate sense.
It will probably resonate immediately with you, and I think you'll know instinctively what I'm talking about – because I'm talking about *you*!

If you're a natural FF, there might not be much that's "new" to you in this chapter, but I hope you'll still find this part of the book useful. As an aspect of *knowing yourself* even better, reading this chapter may well help you to help others whose strengths are oriented differently.

At the very least, you can revel in reading about some of your natural strengths, and hopefully hone them to make them even stronger.

Other readers will be natural *Content-First* types.

If that's you, this chapter may be a bit harder-going.

At times, it'll seem like I'm talking about someone else – because I am!

But please, persevere. Remember, *both mindsets can be learned.*

And there is *so much* to be gained by learning the mindset that isn't your natural preference.

Don't forget: a time-rich life of *smart serendipity* is the goal. Let's take some first steps together on the way!

The first FF key secret perspective: *Time is Mine*

I guess not very many readers will be familiar with the name of Walter W. Skeat.

But in his day, he was a household name.

Skeat was a nineteenth century polymath who taught mathematics at Cambridge University.

For all his broad contribution to knowledge, he was perhaps most famous for his *Etymological Dictionary of the English Language*, first published in 1879.

Skeat wanted to trace the origin of each and every word in his dictionary, but he established a working rule: *he would never spend more than three hours* searching for any one etymology.

After three hours of looking for the origin of some of the more obscure terms in the English language, Skeat would move on, noting the elusive etymologies in his dictionary as "unknown."

You might think that with such an approach, Skeat's dictionary would have lost some authority or appeal. Surely people would have rated it as a second-rate enterprise?

In fact, Skeat's book went through multiple editions, and continues to be enjoyed even today.[4]

William Skeat is an example of an *Form-First* agent in action.

He clearly exhibits the first "key secret perspective" of the FF mindset: *Time is Mine.*

This perspective operates on the **time** dimension.

Remember from chapter 1 my full definition of the *Time is Mine* secret perspective:

> FFs determine how much time and energy to spend on any particular interface by the amount of time they deem to be available, *not* by the supposed "value" of that interface, measured according to any other variable.

How did this work for Skeat? He decided that three hours was the maximum time allowed to search for the etymology of any one word. For example (I've just looked up Skeat's dictionary online) he couldn't find the etymology of the word "parch" (as in, *"I'm parched. Let's have a cuppa."*) Of course, he *could* have kept on searching long beyond three hours, and he might have found the answer. But – and this was Skeat's calculation – *he didn't have the time to do that.*

Crucially, there's nothing special about "three hours." The importance of the etymologies he was researching didn't themselves determine the time Skeat spent on them. Nor was three hours an entirely arbitrary amount of time, chosen at random. Skeat chose three hours because that was the time he had for the job.

Of course, not many of us will write 844-page dictionaries.

So let's think about this might apply to some of the interfaces *you* experience.

When you have a task you have to do, what determines how long you will spend on it? What about a task which has a deadline decided by someone else, like a professor, or client, or boss.

Think back for a minute to that example of an essay or report that you need to submit.

Do you remember that I suggested someone operating with an FF mindset will finish with bags of time to spare?

Why does that happen?

FFs typically decide **before** they begin an interface how long they want to spend on it, and the time *is not determined by how much the interface is "worth"*: *it is determined by how much time they have.*

In fact – and this is so important – it is often determined by how much time *they want* to spend!

A person who operates with an FF mindset decides how much time they want to spend on any particular interface.

If that's an essay or a report, for example, they might decide to spend six hours over three evenings on it. Why? *Not* because they think the essay is "worth" six hours of their time. But because six hours is either the time they *have*, or the time they *want* to spend working on it.

This is why FFs are such *excellent natural time-managers*.

FFs, typically, *don't do* all-nighters.
They *don't do* "last-minute."
Because they don't need to!
Their time is their own.

If you are not naturally an FF, but a *Content-First* (CF) person, what I have just written might strike you as nonsense, or pie-in-the-sky. You might think: surely there aren't people who operate like that? That's because it is quite unnatural for a CF to think and act in these terms.

Perhaps you know someone who always seems to finish things on time or early, and never seems to struggle with deadlines? Maybe that kind of person has made you a bit jealous of their seeming ability to get things done so quickly and efficiently.

Full disclosure: you might have guessed it by now, but I'm an FF, through and through.

I don't think I've ever worked an all-nighter in my life, whether as a student at Cambridge University, as a teacher, as a pastor, or working in financial services.
I usually finish tasks quickly, well before the deadline. I hate being last-minute.

CF friends have often wondered how I make this happen. At university, I remember a friend saying to me, "How come you get such good marks, when you never seem to do any work?"
At the time I wasn't sure. Now I know the answer.
I'm convinced it's got very little to do with IQ or intelligence, and

everything to do with a Form-First mindset.

Here's the secret: when I have to do something, I typically don't think twice about what it's "worth."

I decide how much time to spend on it, and the decision comes from *me*, not from the thing I am doing.

The interface itself does not determine my time. I do.
And so I fit the interface to the time *I've* decided.
Then, I do whatever's necessary to make sure it's finished in time.
My time.
Because *Time is Mine.*

This is what all FFs tend to do – and they tend to do it secretly.
They don't *talk* about it.
They don't particularly *think* about it, at least not in conceptual terms like I'm laying it out for you now.
They might not even be aware that they do it.
That's why their CF friends and colleagues – watching, sometimes enviously – often can't understand *how* FFs do it! We'll see in the next chapter exactly how CFs tend to approach their interfaces, but in short, it's more-or-less the *direct opposite* of the FF mindset.

Anyway, I hope you can see that this key FF secret mindset is *powerful.* It's an approach to your interfaces that puts *you* in the driving-seat.

And once you know the secret (because I've just told it to you!) it's not too difficult to learn how to operate with this key FF perspective in mind.

Okay, it might take a bit of practice, if you're a natural CF.
But you can learn it.

When I first went to live in Japan, I couldn't use chopsticks. Now I can.
Perhaps I don't use chopsticks as well as someone who grew up using them every day as a child. Perhaps I still find using a knife and fork more "natural."
But practically speaking, I can use chopsticks almost as effectively as the next person.
I *learned* how to operate in a different way, with different "tools."
It's the same when you learn the mindset that isn't your natural default.
What I'm doing here is simply giving you the conceptual "tools" to operate according to a new, alternative, mindset.

If CF is your natural preference, why don't you try this with the next task you get?

Instead of thinking about how much the task is "worth" (in terms of its intrinsic value, or the score, or praise, or promotion that you might get from doing it well), start by thinking about *how much time you want to spend on it.*

Once you've decided, why not write it down before you begin:
I will spend 1 hour on this job application.
I want to spend 2 days on this essay.

Or, you could phrase it like this:
I want to finish this PhD within 3 years.
I will research and write this report by 9 p.m. on Tuesday.

When you decide how much time you spend on your interfaces, you are in control.

You can choose how much time to spend, giving yourself some freedom as to when you actually take the time to do it, as in the first two example sentences.

Or you can give yourself a personal "deadline," like in the second two examples.

Note that, in practice, a self-imposed deadline is *nothing like* a real deadline, or a deadline that's imposed on you from outside. It's *self*-imposed, so the only pressure comes from you. And your time is yours.

Ultimately, a self-imposed deadline is flexible, too. After all, the best-laid plans (even of an FF mindset!) do go wrong from time to time.

True, you need to have the self-discipline to meet your deadlines, or at least to aim to meet them so that you make it there most of the time.

If you're lazy, or negligent, none of this will do you much good.

But I'm not for a moment suggesting that *Content-First* people are typically lazy or negligent, while *Form-First* folks are diligent and committed.

It doesn't work like that.

Diligence and effort (and skill) are – as far as I can see – roughly equally divided between FFs and CFs.

The difference is in the *mindset*: in this case the mindset in the **time** dimension.

The key secret perspective *Time is Mine* is only half the story of the FF mindset.

By itself, it's not terribly useful. It might give you the parameters for your next interface.

But it doesn't join up the dots.

If executing an interface on the basis of the FF mindset is like a journey from A to B, then the first key principle – *Time is Mine* – is your compass.

The second key principle, – *Back to Front* – is your map.

The second FF key secret perspective: *Back to Front*

King Abdullah Economic City (or KAEC) is a so-called "megaproject" in Saudi Arabia, due for completion in the year 2020. Situated on the coast of the Red Sea, the city covers 173 km² (66.8 sq mi) and construction has been going on for nearly 15 years. The total cost is projected at SR 207 billion (over £42 billion).

The scale of KAEC is incredible: it is bigger than Washington DC. But here's what makes it special: *it was all planned out from the beginning*, **back to front**.

The designers of KAEC thought first about what they *wanted* (or *needed*) – an industrial zone, sea port, residential areas, sea resort, "educational zone," and a central business district and so on – and *then* they worked out what was required in terms of land, infrastructure, technology, and manpower to give them all of that.

Of course, there were constraints on the project. In oil-rich Saudi Arabia, money isn't too much of a problem! But time and space have certainly been big issues. Even so, KAEC has been constructed more-or-less *according to plan*. That's so different from the way that many of our cities have grown, bit-by-bit, somewhat haphazardly over the years.

KAEC is an example of the second FF key secret perspective, on a massive scale!

In chapter 1, I introduced the perspective:

FFs interface in a primarily *back to forward* direction. That is, they start with an end-game in view, and calculate from there how to engineer the interface in order to arrive at the desired result.

On a more mundane, day-to-day level, this is exactly what FFs do all the time.

Come back to my favourite example – the essay or report you have to do.

When an FF gets a task like that, she doesn't start by thinking about what goes *into* the task: the *content*.

Her first thought is about what the finished task will *look like*, in other words, what *form* it will take.

Is there a particular proforma or template to use? Are there particular rules about submission, or references? If there's a particular word-count, how many pages will that fill? How many chapters will there be?

The typical FF will set up the file with all the correct variables in place before writing anything down.

Next, the person working with an FF mindset will think about the conclusion, or the *final* element of the job in hand.

They may not have thought much at all about the topic itself yet, but if they have *any* idea about it, they'll want to come up with at least an idea of where they're going.

That conclusion might have to be modified as they get into the research or data or whatever, but basically, they know what they are working towards.

Form (structure) comes first: *content* follows.

I hope you can see how this really is a key secret perspective for a smart approach to your tasks and goals. In management-speak, it's known as "backward planning."

Whatever the interface, with both time and space dimensions for any particular project *decided in advance*, FFs are perfectly poised to work quickly and efficiently to their own self-imposed deadlines.

Once again, time-management is their great strength.

Research becomes, for an FF, a way to populate a pre-existing space, rather than the slow "evolution" of form out of a shapeless mass of concepts or data.

Again, this is a "secret" perspective because FFs don't usually make a big thing about it.

But if you want to see it in action, just ask an FF to show you their computer.

You can bet on it: all the files will be ordered. References will be categorised. Notes will be sorted. Templates will be set up. All in the name of *Form-First efficiency*.

Natural CFs will need to work hard at learning this perspective and starting to put it into practice.

If you default to the CF mindset, next time you begin working on a task, give the FF approach a try!

You will probably find it feels most unnatural at first.

You might well wonder: *How can you know what something will look like when it's finished, if you don't yet know what "something" is?*

Experience is the key.

Essays and work projects, whatever they're about, don't really vary too much in form.

So, get the form sorted *first.*

And then learn to apply the form before you move on to the content.

I have seen many PhD students (surely CFs!) "finish" their theses, only to find that they haven't formatted their references properly, because they didn't bother to check the rules in advance and set the defaults on their software correctly. These people then spend days (weeks, in some cases!) trying to sort out the resulting mess, when they could have been finished. Usually, these people have already taken much longer to finish than an FF would anyway, because they haven't operated time-efficiently. They haven't applied the first key secret perspective of the FF mindset.

In my interfaces, as a natural FF, I tend to work "back to front."

One of the great gains is that I don't waste much time on things that will never be relevant to the final work.

I don't write chapters that I later discard.

I don't go down rabbit-holes, chasing pointless bits of information.

I know where I need to go, and I can get there with the minimum of fuss, and only the effort that's absolutely necessary.

I make the space that I fill.

The space is mine, and it stretches out to a horizon that I have laid.

I have control over my interfaces.

If FF is your natural preference, I'm sure you will recognise this sense of empowerment.

Be thankful, for you have a great skill!

On the other hand, if you prefer a CF mindset by nature it's more likely your experience that the horizon doesn't tend to "appear" for you until a project or job begins to crystallise in your mind. Then, and only then, you feel that you can start to put a form or structure on it.

There's a great loss of time and energy in such an approach.

If you can begin to learn the FF mindset, and put into practice the two key secret principles I have outlined in this chapter, I'm confident that you will find yourself with significantly more time for the things that really matter to you.

One change you'll notice is that you'll start to share in some of the *typical characteristics* of FFs, which we'll look at now.

Four typical characteristics of FFs

What are *Form-First* types like? In this section, I'll highlight four typical characteristics, alongside the contrasting (or complementary) traits of typical CFs. Two quick general points about these:

First, I want you to notice that all four of these are (or can be) **positive** characteristics. It's not that one is good and its opposite number is bad. Rather, each is demanded at different times, by different interfaces. That's why we really need to be able to function with both mindsets.

Second, any and all of these characteristics can be **learned**. In other words, they are not the sole preserve of "natural" FFs. If your preferred mindset is CF, you can still develop these characteristics. The way to do that is by practising the key secret perspectives of FFs outlined above.

So, FFs are typically…

Finishers rather than perfectionists

FFs excel at *getting things done*. I think this is the single most important characteristic of the FF mindset, so I'll spend a bit more time on this one than the others.

FFs can finish tasks at great speed, with maximum efficiency.

They are people who know how to seal the proverbial deal, without the faff and flannel.

Whenever they can help it, they don't leave loose ends.

Completing an interface is very important to FFs.

As we've seen above, FFs operate with a "back to front" perspective.

They begin with the end-game, and work back from there so that their steps and progress are logical, calculated, and efficient, always with a clear goal in view.

They know what they want, and they set out to get it.

We've also seen how FFs have a key secret *Time is Mine* perspective.

This is crucial to their strategic finishing ability. FFs like to determine when they will finish before they've even started.

If you're *not* good at finishing what you've started, or at finishing things on time, *surely you would like to be!*

But how can you develop this characteristic?

The answer is simple. It's the same with all these four characteristics: by learning the key secret perspectives of FFs, in the two dimensions of **time** and **space**.

It's no more complicated than this: *Time is Mine*, and *Back to Front!*

If you put these principles into practice, I promise you that you will become more and more of a finisher.

Let me just clear up here a common misunderstanding that sometimes arises at this point. The misunderstanding is that I'm advocating something sub-optimal, like *get it finished at all costs!* It sounds to some people that the "finisher" I'm describing must be willing to make significant compromises in quality just in order to get to the finish line.

In fact, some books on efficiency or time-management **do** advocate this sort of approach. It's not unusual to hear maxims for promoting efficiency such as *Aim for 80%*.

I can understand why this sort of principle sounds like it might be a good idea. As we'll see later on, the *Content-First* mindset is highly perfectionist. Aiming for four-fifths sounds like a reasonable way to curb the CF tendency to keep on going and going in search of unattainable perfection.

But I think it's a wrong-headed approach. A better maxim would be **good enough is good enough**. In the FF mindset, what is "good enough," remember, is fundamentally determined by *me*.

Of course, there are usually external constraints. I can't just "decide" that a 'D' grade is good enough if an examiner deems it to be a failure. But I am still the arbiter of my ultimate goals. *By definition*, my "good enough" is 100%.

Please don't think for a moment that the FF mindset is a short-cut to mediocrity. It is anything but that! It is not a "short-cut" to anywhere. It is a *mindset*, a way of interfacing with the world, that is *excellent* and *optimal* in certain situations. It is the *best* way of getting certain things done, of the very highest quality.

So, there's no encouragement here for you to settle for second best. *Always aim for 100%!* Good enough is good enough. In other words, there's no point in aiming for, or producing something that's 120%. If good enough is good enough, and good enough is *by definition* 100%, you've just wasted 20% time and effort.

Learn to be a finisher. Get your *form* in place first – *time* and *space*. And you'll be able to deliver.

What are some other characteristics of the FF mindset?

Realists rather than idealists

FFs are naturally attuned to the art of the *possible*. They may well be principled and passionate people, too. But they will relentlessly pursue *achievable* goals.

We're all familiar with the dreamer-type, whose head is up in the clouds and who has a poor grasp of the constraints of the real world.

FFs are the exact opposite: down to earth and realistic.

FFs typically have a great understanding of, and affinity for, **systems**. If they don't *create* the system themselves, they will quickly *learn* the system, and figure out the most effective way to harness it to their own advantage. They are good at working with external constraints and exploiting external opportunities.

FFs are often highly aware of their own **personal limitations**. For that reason, they won't set the bar too high. They won't bite off more than they can chew. They know that there are only 24 hours in the day. They are sanguine about their own capabilities. So, when setting goals and deadlines, they are good at working with internal constraints and exploiting internal opportunities.

One practical implication of this realism is that there's a lot that FFs just won't take on in the first place. If they know they probably can't *finish* it (at least not without a *lot* of unnecessary stress) they probably won't *start* it.

I've had many colleagues over the years who have been swamped with work some weeks, while seemingly kicking their heels at other times. I call this "fried-diary syndrome." Of course, most jobs have their seasons. When I was a tax accountant in the City of London, there was a particularly busy time in January each year when the tax filing deadlines came along. At those times, it was "all hands on deck," with late evenings and weekend work. But that was the exception.

I strongly suspect that my colleagues who suffered from "fried-diary syndrome" were *Content-First* folks. They accepted jobs without a realistic assessment of constraints of time and ability. And they paid the price when the deadlines came around. (They probably made things worse by not adopting the *Time is Mine* and *Back to Front* perspectives that come naturally to FFs.)

FFs also pay attention to how **other people** both contribute to, and potentially damage, their interfaces. Of course, they don't know others as well as they know themselves. There are inevitably a lot of variables here. But FFs are aware of the variables, and they put strategies in place to manage them. They can be effective bosses and managers, communicating ideas succinctly and persuasively, and motivating staff to work for them with clear expectations about what needs to be done.

Realistic awareness of the limitations and opportunities inherent in systems, self, and other people: this characteristic of **realism** is typical of FFs. It's a strength of self-awareness and sensitivity. Of course, it's a great advantage to anyone who can possess it at the right time.

But how do you develop it? Again, this is not as complicated as you might think. It comes to you in just the same way as you learn to be a *finisher*: you simply need to put into practice the two key secret perspectives of the FF mindset: *time is mine*, and *back to front*.

You see, when you operate according to the perspectives *time is mine* and *back to front*, you're automatically in the *real* world. You're making decisions about *real* time, *real* space, and *real* people, yourself included. There's no leeway to drift off into escapism or unreality. If you set the form and structure of your interfaces in places *first*, you'll find that realism does begin to come "naturally" to you, even if FF is not your preferred default mindset.

Conventional rather than innovative

Being "conventional" gets a bad press. Synonyms include "everyday," "straight," "commonplace," and "square."

But conventional needn't mean "boring" or "straitjacketed."

Things, especially systems, formats, and processes, are very often "correct," "established," and "prevalent" for a very good reason – they *work*!

The FF mindset thrives on repetition and ritual. Like a well-oiled machine, it revels in learning to do things, and to do them *very well*.

When I was at school, I did well in public exams. And I didn't work particularly hard, either. I'm not telling you that to boast about it. (Who boasts about school exams, anyway?) I'm telling you that because I'm convinced this was largely the fruit of applying my natural FF mindset.

Rather than focusing on all the *stuff* I needed to learn for each test, I focused my attention on the *tests* themselves.

In other words, I mastered an exam technique. I only had to learn one.
I learned about things like question selection, time keeping, and structure. I developed a strategy – a convention – for taking exams.

All exams are basically the same. There's no need to re-invent the wheel every time.

Some of my peers, who were very clever, but most likely default CFs, spent *countless hours* on study and revision and, in most cases, they didn't end up doing any better than I did.
Their problem was – they were methodological innovators. One approach for every subject.

The FF mindset is naturally systematising. It looks for, and finds, *patterns* rather than *variations*. It is order-loving, and appreciates the beauty and efficiency of the tried-and-tested.

This kind of "conventionality" is powerful. It doesn't need to mean that FFs are short-sighted, or narrow-minded, or that they don't have new ideas. FFs just as often create their own conventions as submit to the conventions of others.

But their key characteristic is this: once they've found a convention that *works for them*, they stick with it, refine it, and hone it to perfection.

This isn't the natural default of my CF friends. CFs prefer to approach each interface with, as it were, a blank slate. As we've seen above FFs will format their work *before* they start, usually gravitating to a "favourite" format. Ask an FF what font they prefer, and they'll typically tell you they use the same one over and over.

CFs, on the other hand, format their work *last*. CFs are always tinkering with the little details, experimenting with new fonts or formats or fine points, and feeling their way towards a structure, which only emerges right at the end.

Again, if you're a natural CF but you're now convinced of the value of the FF mindset for some of your interfaces, I think you'll want to learn to display the characteristic of conventionality.

Remember, it will come out as you put into practice the two key secret perspectives of the FF mindset: *time is mine*, and *back to front*.

The FF mindset is an interface-*owner*. FF's "boss" their interfaces, across the two dimensions of time and space. The FF mindset is also an interface-*repeater*, building on successes by applying tried-and-tested formulae to life's challenges.

Of course, FFs have failures. I've experienced many myself. When I was at Cambridge University, my graduation dissertation got a 2:2 grade. I was gutted. I've had multiple academic articles rejected by peer-reviewed journals. Rejection is never easy. In the City, I once made such a careless error of judgment at work that the head of our department never spoke a civil word to me again. I've suffered a total relationship breakdown with another boss who was controlling and unable to communicate effectively. I can hardly claim that I "bossed" these interfaces!

But you don't need me to tell you that failures can make you stronger. FFs, at their best, can learn to turn their experiences of failure to their advantage, and feed them into the development of better and more robust conventions that will work for them into the future.

To be clear, I'm not saying that FFs don't, or can't, or shouldn't, innovate. But their characteristic is to innovate with a specific purpose in mind: to build conventions – systems, formats, and processes – that *work for them.*

Strategic rather than spontaneous

We've seen that the FF mindset exemplifies a *realistic, convention*-based approach to interfaces, which gets things *finished*. A related characteristic of FFs (which in some ways grounds all the others) is that they are *strategic*.

The ancient Greek word *strategos*, which gives us our English *strategy* and *strategic*, meant "military general." The *strategos* would marshall his troops (sorry, girls, but Greek *strategoi* were invariably men!), choose his ground, pick his moment, and execute his battle-plan.

In a similar way, the FF today marshalls her "troops" (with a realistic assessment of the resources and abilities available to her), chooses her "ground" (as she "bosses" the *space* dimension with her preferred format), picks her moment (in the *time* dimension, determining her own parameters for finishing), and executes her well-honed "battle-plan" for successful interfaces.

In all their interfaces, FFs are the *commanders* of time and space!

Unlike the generals of the First World War, who famously made their decisions far from the Front Line, moving battalions of troops like pawns on a chess-board, FFs lead from the front, taking the strategic initiative in their interfaces, and so staying one step ahead of the game.

All this is mostly foreign to the *Content-First* mindset. Because CFs tend to allow parameters of time and space to be determined by their interfaces, they are instinctively less strategic.

A CF who wants to exhibit strategic strength needs, as always, to develop the two key secret perspectives of the FF mindset: *Time is Mine* and *Back to Front*.

General George S. Patton was one of the most important American military commanders during World War II. He was known for his brilliance on the battlefield, and his studious avoidance of "paralysis by analysis."

George Patton was a classic FF. One of his best-known quotes is, "A good plan, violently executed now, is better than a perfect plan next week." This might well be the motto of the FF mindset! Patton worked on the basis that good enough is good enough. He knew that he needed a plan for the *here-and-now*, and he bossed the dimensions of time and space to put one together. He was relentless in "violent execution" of his plans.

Some readers may object to the military idiom, but of course I mean you to imitate it only metaphorically. Patton *seized the moment of his own choosing*. He was enough of a realist to avoid the mythical "perfect plan next week." He acted on the basis of his rich experience, building on his own well-worn and tried-and-tested conventions, with the flexibility to modify his plans in the heat of battle. Above all, Patton was a *strategist*. FFs follow in his footsteps.

Weaknesses of the FF mindset

It's time for a brief recap. In this chapter we've been looking in depth at the *Form-First* (FF) mindset, one of the two basic mindsets with which we human beings operate when we engage with the world.

Some readers will have FF as their natural default mindset. They will doubtless have been reading this chapter with plenty of recognition and quite likely a bit of pride in their own favoured approach. That's fine. The FF mindset is *powerful*, and *essential* if we are to master our interfaces on the way to *time-rich living*.

The FF mindset is the foundation of the "smartness" that makes *smart serendipity* the model for the time-rich life.

But, before FFs get carried away with themselves, and head off to "boss" some more interfaces, *remember*! The FF mindset is *only half of the story*. There are **two** basic mindsets, and without adopting **both** of them, we will never be truly time-rich.

That's because there are certain interfaces for which the FF mindset is without doubt sub-optimal. These include the following:

· *Relaxing*

The FF mindset typically operates on high-alert. So FFs struggle to wind down. They try to "boss" their down-time as much as their up-time, but end up unable to relax, always trying (subconsciously) to impose form on what needs to remain formless, or feeling guilty about being cut off from "productive" tasks. Any interface without defined dimensions (time and space) is a likely area of weakness for the FF mindset.

· Open-ended social encounters

FFs like to focus on the end-game. Anything open-ended is particularly stressful for the FF mindset, which instinctively wants to set space and time parameters on all its interfaces. This is worse than unhelpful in many of our relationships. FFs can struggle in making and maintaining close friendships, or in communication within marriage or other long-term relationships. Teamwork may also fall within this category, especially if the FF is not the team leader, or the person calling the shots.

· Creative pursuits

Always with one eye on the bottom line, or the next deliverable, FFs are not naturally suited to engaging in creative pursuits where there is no clear plan in view. Such pursuits might include activities as varied as going for a walk without a particular purpose, discussions without a clear focus, or creative/artistic projects in which the end point is not obvious.

· Open-minded, or so called "blue-sky" thinking

Similarly, FFs typically don't like the kind of thinking where parameters are removed. They may be strong at problem-solving, even *creative* problem-solving when all the variables are known. But they do not do well when there are many "unknowns" or they are asked to suspend judgment. Meditation (such as is recommended in so-called "mindfulness") is not something that comes naturally to the FF mindset.

· Awareness and appreciation of being in "the moment"

Because FFs prefer the "time is mine" and "back to front" approach to their interfaces, they are always thinking ahead. It is very hard to get the FF mindset to slow down and be aware of the present. FFs *may* have good social intelligence (in that they can empathise and understand the effects of their actions on others) but this does not usually translate into good "presence" for the typical FF.

What all of this means is that, while FFs may exhibit consummate *smartness*, they are often closed to *serendipity*. Theirs is a *search* approach to life, with little space left for *surfing*.

This is ironic. FFs typically have "more" time than CFs, precisely because they *boss* their time – it's their own. But FFs who haven't developed CF mindset as a second operating mindset for certain interfaces are *not truly time-rich.*

If you're an FF by nature, and you've read this far, I hope you can see that your default mindset isn't always optimal. There are some significant weaknesses to it. You need to cultivate the CF mindset as well. In the next chapter, I'll tell you how.

If you have a natural CF preference, I'm pretty sure you'll have found this chapter a challenge at times. But I want to encourage you again that it's not too difficult to learn the FF mindset. Now that you know the two key secret perspectives of the FF mindset, you can begin to apply them to your interfaces. Good luck!

Of course, the question remains: which interfaces demand an FF approach, and which require the CF mindset? That discernment question will be the subject of chapter 4. First, though, let's get stuck into the *Content-First* mindset.

3 THE CONTENT-FIRST MINDSET

"Serendipity will take you beyond the currents of what is familiar.
Invite it. Watch for it. Allow it."
· Jeanne McElvaney

"Serendipity happens when a well-trained mind looking for one things encounters
something else: the unexpected."
· Margot Lee Shetterly, *Hidden Figures*

This chapter is all about the *Content-First* (CF) mindset.

If you've already read chapter two, on the *Form-First* mindset, you'll have some idea of where we'll be going. (FFs will appreciate that sort of foreknowledge!)

If you've skipped chapter two for now because you wanted to begin here (whether or not CF is your natural preference) *welcome*!

Following a similar structure to the previous chapter, I'll explain here in detail what the CF mindset is, how it works, and how to develop it, again with real-life examples and comparisons so that you can clearly see what I'm talking about.

Remember, CF is one of the two basic mindsets that we all need to learn, in order to enjoy *time-rich living*.

The CF mindset is the path to the "serendipity" aspect of *smart serendipity*.

Back in chapter 1, we saw that there are two types of people in the world.

Some readers – natural CFs – will probably feel right at home in this chapter: like a fish *in* water!

This will feel like home territory, as I discuss what's familiar, instinctive, and safe.

Other readers will be natural *Form-First* types.

If you've already read chapter two, you'll know that I'm one of you!

Not only is this chapter probably harder to *read*, *digest*, and *implement* for those who default to the FF mindset, it was harder to *write* for me – a natural FF.

But it's my experience that it's possible to learn another mindset. It may take years to perfect it, but the basic moves (I call them the *key secret perspectives*) are actually quite simple to grasp and to act on.

And remember: there is *so much* to be gained by learning the mindset that isn't your natural preference.

Don't forget: a time-rich life of *smart serendipity* is our shared goal. Let's take a few more steps together on the way!

The first CF key secret perspective: *My Time is Yours*

In Tolkien's classic *The Lord of the Rings*, Sam Gamgee makes a promise that he will never leave Frodo Baggins, come what may. Sam doesn't know at this stage in the story exactly what lies ahead: danger, destruction, possible death, and a six-month journey to Mount Doom. But he makes a commitment to Frodo, knowing the importance of the great quest with which his master and friend has been entrusted. And Sam is faithful to his promise.

Sam Gamgee may be a fictional character, but he exemplifies the first key secret perspective of the *Content-First* mindset – *My Time is Yours*.

In chapter one I summarised it like this:

> CFs determine how much time and energy to spend on any particular interface by the "value" they attach to that interface. The value, however it is determined, is thought to be something that inheres, objectively, *in* the interface. It does not primarily depend on the

situation of the CF who interfaces with it.

For Sam, Frodo *is* the most important interface. Everything else that happens to them on the way to Mount Doom – every other interface – is relative to this *personal* one.

The CF mindset defaults to establishing *open-ended interfaces.*
It willingly (consciously or not) *hands over* the determination of time to something or someone else.

If you've read chapter two, you'll know that this is the reason why CFs appear to be poor at time-management. They tend to start tasks without thinking about how and when they'll get them finished. They allow others (other people, or other things) to determine their deadlines.

But there's a flipside to this, and the flipside is profoundly positive.

Content-First people are able to ascribe value to their interfaces, based on a real assessment of *what the interface is worth in itself.*

They open themselves – heart and mind – to their interfaces.

CFs are naturally loyal servants. Whatever (or whoever) has their attention, they give their time to it. They give *themselves.*

Incidentally, this is one reason why I think CF types are possibly more susceptible to addictions such as alcohol, gambling, or pornography.

But – and remember our focus is on the positives here – this willingness to give time to others, to "lose control" of their time for the sake of projects that they believe are worthwhile or worthy, is a great treasure!

If a CF decides that an interface is valuable, she will hold on to it, and resist letting it go with all her strength. She won't "count the cost" in advance.

In personal relationships, this is an invaluable mindset, and CFs have it naturally. In friendships and romantic relationships, CFs will typically pour themselves out for the other person, always willing to give of their time and energies.

There are some differences in the way this works for introverted and extraverted CFs, but the basic mindset is the same. There's no prior reckoning. No asking, "When will this be finished?" or "What am I trying to get out of this?" or "What's the deliverable here?"

It may sound as though the CF mindset is merely *passive*, in response to the *active* FF mindset. But that's not quite right. CFs can be just as active, in their own way. But the engine-room that drives their activity seems to be located in a different place. It is almost as though CFs are driven by their hearts, rather than their heads. But even that isn't the whole truth.

A CF is able to make a determination of the value of any particular interface *just as rationally* as any FF.

The difference is that the value is not so much determined *internally* (by the CF person and his own constraints) as *externally* (by the presenting interface).

Here's an example. Mary Robinson, former President of Ireland, served as United Nations High Commissioner for Human Rights from 1997-2002. Her personal passion for the issues surrounding human rights made her a tireless campaigner for causes close to her heart. In more recent years, she has taken on the cause of climate change, and has become a voice advocating for global justice for the poor, the disempowered, and the marginalised victims of global warming.

Robinson's career choices have been characterised by the CF mindset. She has chosen to support particular causes, not primarily for emotive reasons, but because she sees their *intrinsic* importance. On this basis, she has *ascribed value* to them, and has given her time to them.

The causes she has supported have been open-ended ones, certainly without easy answers, and in many cases lacking obvious deliverables. But she has been a *tireless campaigner* in support of these causes. Any time you hear someone referred to as a *tireless campaigner*, there's a good chance you're dealing with the CF mindset in action. CFs say to their chosen interfaces: *My Time is Yours.*

The CF mindset excels in the search for truth, goodness, and beauty that characterises (or should characterise) our lives as human beings. This is because of its open-ended approach to allocating time and effort – an approach that is necessary for, and perfectly suited to, such a search.

CFs will pursue ideas, thoughts, intuitions, conversations, and concepts – and continue seeking until they find satisfying answers to the questions they have. They will rarely be content with soundbites or pat solutions that don't deal with the complexities of life.

To some extent, the FF mindset "pursues ideas" as well. But it looks quite different.

Remember the *search* and *surf* distinction I introduced in chapter 1. Just as there are two different ways of using the internet, so there are two different ways of engaging the world: *search* and *surf.*

The FF mindset is primarily a *search* mindset. It might sound at times like FFs are on a quest. And they are, sort of. But the typical FF approach to a quest is to "boss" it, by determining its parameters in advance, especially how much time it will take. FFs put *form* first, and only then do they think about *content.*

CFs are quite different. Because theirs is first-and-foremost a *surf* mentality, they embark on a quest without deciding a finishing-point. This means that they are *open to serendipity. Content* comes first: *Form* follows later.

Because they don't limit the timeframe of their interfaces in advance, CFs are amenable to changes of direction, changes of pace, and even changes of the entire interface! When it comes to the big questions in life – truth, goodness, and beauty – CFs are *open-minded.*

That doesn't mean that a CF needs to (or will) spend all their life looking for these things without ever settling on something. Quite often, the CF will *find* what they are looking for. Having ascribed value to their (inherently valuable) findings, CFs will then "serve" the things they find – pursuing truth, goodness and beauty in their own lives, and taking every opportunity to share their findings with others.

All this means that CFs are geared towards receiving life's riches – especially the unexpected ones that come via *serendipity.* Of course, you'll see I'm not talking about *financial* riches here. Perhaps some people do come into great financial wealth because of their openness to serendipity, but having a default CF mindset is no short cut to winning the lottery! The riches I'm referring to are the riches of a truly *time-rich life.*

The CF mindset is open to the riches that makes our time truly *rich.* In opening ourselves to other people, to valuable causes, and to the quest for truth, goodness, and beauty, we open ourselves up to *rich* time. This might be as simple and everyday as the way we relate to our partner or children, or to colleagues at work. Or it could be as extraordinary and life-defining as the discovery of a cause that we give our heart to, for the sake of others as well as ourselves.

If you're a default CF, I guess you will resonate with what I'm talking about. Something about it will make your heart beat stronger: *instinctively* you sense that this is what life is all about! Be thankful that you have this natural strength when it comes to your interfaces with the world. It's a precious gift!

As I've said, I'm a natural FF. The CF perspective isn't my natural default. I've had to learn it. I'm still learning it. So, if you're like me, how can you start to acquire the CF mindset as a second way of interfacing?

All you need to do to start enjoying richer time is to adopt the first key secret perspective of the CF mindset: *My Time is Yours*.

I say, "*all* you need to do." But of course, it's a challenge, if you have a natural preference for form over content like I have. The FF perspective is *Time is Mine*. As we've seen in chapter two, *Time is Mine* is a great perspective for some interfaces. But not for all.

So, here's a first simple step. Think of a relationship that you have: with a family member, or a colleague, or a friend. To make it a bit easier, make it someone you like! Now, next time you see that person, consciously tell yourself: *My Time is Yours*. You don't have to say it to them. They might think you're a bit strange if you do. But try to act like you mean it. Make the time open-ended. Perhaps, don't even decide in advance what you're going to do, or say. Certainly, be open to letting the other person set the agenda.

I try to put this into practice with my children. It's not easy, because it doesn't come naturally to me. But the simple perspective – *My Time is Yours* – makes all the difference in the world. I'm open to them. I'm ready to "serve" them. I'm open to serendipity.

You *can* learn a mindset that's not your own. Speaking as a parent, I'd say that having children often *forces* an FF (in a good way!) to learn the CF mindset. You *can't* keep on saying to your kids, *Time is Mine*. At least if you *keep* thinking and acting in that way, you're probably heading for trouble.

But you don't need to have children to learn the CF mindset in your relationships. You could try giving some time for volunteering. Or just spend more open-ended time with your parents or friends. Whatever you do, try to keep the perspective in mind: *My Time is Yours.*

The CF mindset isn't just for relationship-type interfaces, as we've seen. There may be no better place to learn the CF mindset than in a library. For a few years now, I've committed myself to going to the public library on the way home from work, at least once a week. Sometimes it's just for 10 minutes. Other days I will take longer, or bring something home with me.

Libraries are where serendipity *happens*. As children's author Lemony Snicket says, "With a library it is easier to hope for serendipity than to look for a precise answer." *Libraries are places to surf, as well as to search.*

So don't go looking for a particular thing. Go to the library to *surf*, and you will be surprised what you find. If you find that you naturally gravitate towards a particular section of the library, make a conscious decision to go somewhere else. If American fiction is your thing, try gardening. If you prefer self-help books, have a go at poetry. Another author, Penelope Lively, sums up what I'm saying: "Libraries favour serendipity, invite it; the roaming along a shelf, eyeing an unfamiliar name, taking this down, then that – oh, who's this? Never heard of her – give her a go? That is where, and how, you learn affinity and rejection. You find out what you like by exploring what you do not."

And remember, your mindset when you enter the library is *My Time is Yours.*
Rich time awaits you!

So much for the CF mindset in the *time* dimension. Now, let's consider its relation to *space*.

The second CF key secret perspective: *Front to Back*

The story of the 5th-century BC Persian Queen Esther is one of the best loved "comedies" of antiquity. It's a "comedy," not in the sense that we often use that word today (for something that makes you laugh) but as a piece of literature (like we call Shakespeare's play *A Midsummer Night's Dream* a "comedy") – amusing, satirical, with a happy ending.

In the story, Esther is a poor girl from an ethnic minority (the Jews), living under the rule of the greatest world empire of the day. The King, Xerxes, decides he wants a new wife after his previous one "insults" him publicly. Xerxes puts on a nationwide beauty contest. Young women from all across the empire are brought to the capital, Susa, for a whole year of beauty treatments, before being brought to the king.

When Esther is chosen by the king as his new wife, she is suddenly lifted up to a place of prominence and potential power. As the story goes on, Esther has the opportunity to take a great risk: she may be able to save her own Jewish people, but she might lose everything, including her own life, in the endeavour. In the end, Esther is successful: her people are spared, while their enemies are punished. As I said, it's a happy ending!

But one of the striking things about Esther's story is that none of it seems to be planned or premeditated. Until the very end, Esther doesn't "boss" events. She seems to be at the mercy of things that happen to her, and of others who apparently control her destiny.

Yet she is ultimately successful – and serendipitously so!

In one of the best known lines in the story, Esther's uncle Mordecai says to her, "Who knows but that you have come to your royal position for such a time as this?" Who knows, indeed! The book of Esther doesn't mention God, although his involvement (and knowledge) is surely implied. But the point is that none of the human characters in the story – including Esther – know *why* Esther has become queen!

Whether by design or by necessity, Esther has to "make it up" as she goes along. She is an example of the CF mindset in action, working in the *space* dimension from *Front to Back*.

In chapter 1, I introduced this second key secret characteristic of the CF mindset:

> CFs interface in a primarily *front to back* direction. That is, they start with where they are, and move forward incrementally, with a high level of openness to changing direction or even finishing without a resolution of any sort, if circumstances demand that.

This is how Esther operated in her interfaces. Only at the very end of the story does Esther take matters definitely into her own hands. (I like to think she learned to operate in her non-dominant mindset!) For the most part, she takes things a step at a time, changing direction when necessary.

Now, we need to be a bit careful here. Esther lived in a time when it was "acceptable" for kings to have vast harems, and when women typically had very little power.

I'm not suggesting for a moment that those aspects of Esther's story are praiseworthy. To some extent, Esther was *unable* to "boss" her space.

But even today, there are many spaces in our lives we can't "boss," and it's healthy to recognise that, like Esther did.

There are aspects of our lives, and interfaces we are confronted with, where it pays to be open-ended. We've already seen that in the *time* dimension: *My Time is Yours*. But it's true in the *space* dimension too.

Those who default to the CF mindset tend to allow *content* to shape their interfaces. If they're working on a written project, for example, they won't determine in advance what the project will look like – how many chapters it will have, how the segues will join one section to another, what the conclusion might say, and so on. Instead, they will just *begin research*.

CFs are *data*-driven. Their projects only take shape right at the end. Sometimes things don't take shape at all, and that's okay for a CF. CFs would usually rather leave something unfinished than complete something that they don't think does justice to the subject. As we've seen in chapter two, this is why CFs are often last-minute people. The value of their interfaces is determined by something which they identify as inherent in the interface itself.

But there are many interfaces for which the CF mindset is the optimal approach.

For example, there are some things we do in life which simply *cannot* be formally determined ahead of time.

One of these things is starting a family. My sister is a natural CF. She's the polar opposite of me in this respect. And she's a natural when it comes to dealing with the uncertainties of family life. At one point, she had "3 under 3" (three kids under the age of three) and life at home was bordering on chaos! But my sister has no problem with beginning each day with where she is, moving forward incrementally, with a high level of openness to changing direction. CFs like my sister are really good at this.

Her husband (my brother-in-law), on the other hand, is the *ultimate* natural FF. If it's possible, he's more of an FF than I am. He's the kind of guy who had his whole life planned out on an Excel file, literally! And then his wife got pregnant with twins! That was five years ago, and since then my brother-in-law has *had* to learn to operate with a CF mindset. It may not come naturally to him, but I reckon he's done admirably!

My wife and I haven't had twins, but we're both default FFs and in our own way we've both had to learn to develop a secondary CF mindset for raising a family.

However, family life isn't the only context that presents us with CF-optimised interfaces.
There are some work projects that we do which are best done according to CF perspectives, open to the serendipity that comes with them.

One example is *networking*. You can be quite proactive about networking, of course. But by definition you don't know quite who you're going to meet, or who you're going to hit it off with, or which connections will bear fruit in the longer term. It's a serendipitous, *surfing*, endeavour. Content should take precedence over form.

Also, most of us will experience in our workplaces from time to time some projects that demand we hold form in abeyance, at least until the content gives us a hint about what the form should look like.

Management consultants are the professionals when it comes to these sorts of projects. When I worked in a 900-member church in central Oxford, with a staff of about thirty, we called in a church consultant to give us advice on our procedures and structure. The consultant had never been to our church before, and so he came with relatively few preconceived ideas. He spent his first few days interviewing a wide cross-section of "stakeholders": staff at all levels, church members, and others who accessed our programmes. He asked probing questions about the current structures and exactly how things worked.

A few weeks later he sent us his written report and recommendations. It was an eye-opening exercise. The consultant first looked at what we *did* as a church, on the ground. He worked out what was important to us, in terms of what we were doing and how we were doing it, trying hard to get beneath the outward "forms" to the ideas and values (the "content") that undergirded them. Starting from there, he offered his advice about structures. As a result of the report, we implemented some significant changes, most of which led to improvements in how we operated as an organisation. I was really impressed with the consultant's work.

This kind of project demands a CF mindset.

If you naturally default to the CF mindset, I'm pretty sure that projects like this will be appealing to you. You like to get a hold on all the relevant data before you commit yourself. You're willing to think outside the box about structures and forms, and bring them into an interface at a later stage, once the content has dictated what they might be. Having this mindset is a real strength.

Needless to say, it's not the kind of work that a natural FF gravitates towards. And the FF mindset is ill-suited to getting optimal results in projects like these.

So, if you're a default FF, what can you do to develop a CF mindset for those times when its required?

My advice is simple: learn the second key secret characteristic of the FF mindset: *Front to Back*.

When you approach an interface, don't try to pre-empt or pre-determine it.
Allow the material to draw you in. And let the form come later. *Surf!*

When you adopt the CF mindset, the future is full of unknowns, but each unknown is pregnant with possibilities. Every day, every encounter, every idea – each one is a new opportunity.

With a CF approach to life as a whole, the process of readjustment and recalibration never really ends. Even once your course is "set," there remains an openness to whatever might come along.

If you can begin to learn the CF mindset, and put into practice the two key secret principles I have shared in this chapter, I'm confident that you will find your time is *richer* for it.

One change I'm sure you'll notice is that you'll start to share in some of the typical characteristics of CFs, which we'll consider next.

Four typical characteristics of CFs

What are *Content-First* types like? In this section, I'll highlight four typical characteristics, along with the contrasting (or complementary) traits of typical FFs. If you've already read chapter two, some of these ideas may sound familiar, but here we'll be approaching them from the opposite perspective.

Seeing things from two different perspectives is part of the necessary discernment we need to decide *which* mindset is appropriate *when*: you might consider this section a bit of useful practice for what I'll develop in more depth in chapter 4.

Remember: all four characteristics here are (or can be) **positive**. It's not that one is good and its opposite number is bad. Rather, each is demanded at different times, by different interfaces. That's why we really need to be able to function with both mindsets.

And, as before, any of these characteristics can be **learned**. In other words, they are not the sole preserve of "natural" CFs. If you are a default FF like I am, you can still develop these characteristics. The way to do that is by practising the key secret perspectives of CFs outlined above.

So, CFs are typically...

Perfectionists rather than finishers

Whatever CFs do, they give their all to it. It's not just that they have a natural inclination to give limitless time and effort to their interfaces (until deadlines or other constraints are imposed on them from outside). They will seek *perfection*.

For the CF mindset, *fullness* trumps *finishing*. *Being* complete is more important than actually complet*ing*. CFs won't rush things unless they have to. (They invariably *do* rush when they *do* have to, typically up to the very last minute!)

You can usually tell a natural CF child by looking at his school projects – (of course, his parents may have had some input too!) CFs will produce work with bells and whistles. They'll often exceed others' expectations, and find insights and applications that no-one else has considered.
They are thorough, and thoroughly committed.

In their relationships, also, CFs are perfectionist, but (ideally) without the negative connotations that this word sometimes carries. You see, it's not that CFs necessarily try to fit others into their own moulds, or that CFs put impossibly high standards on themselves or other people. CFs are actually, in their own way, typically *more comfortable* with relationship "mess" and struggles than FFs are. Remember that CFs are not too worried about "losing control" of their interfaces, at least temporarily.

The relationship "perfectionism" that I'm talking about is much more healthy than any of these controlling impulses. CFs work with what they've got, and they don't give up on it. They will willingly spend long hours on sorting out differences. They'll go the extra mile to make the other person the centre of their attention. They are often open to trying new ideas and patterns of interacting in order to deal with any problems in their relationships, rather than falling into the same old ruts again and again.

What this means is that CFs are usually good at making, and keeping, friendships. For the CF herself, the benefit is not just that stronger relationships are often the result. As far as our human interfaces go, the *deeper* you dig, the *richer* the minerals you can potentially mine. This is true of relationship interfaces. And it's true of many other things we do at work or in our personal lives.

CFs experience *richness* in their interfaces.

Their pursuit of perfection isn't stifling or threatening. It's open, persistent, and hopeful.

At this point, let me tell you a couple of secrets about my own type – *Form First*. Many FFs have the bad habit of tending to look down at CFs half the time. We notice them scrambling to make deadlines and observe what looks like the chaos in their lives, and we're secretly glad that we don't have to put up with all of that mess!

We can see that so many CFs are *not time-rich*.

But that's only half the story. The other half of the time, we look at CFs and we're full of *admiration* (on our good days) or *envy* (on our bad ones). That's because we sense that they're on to something! Their pursuit of perfectionism – their unwillingness to say that *good enough is good enough* – means that they keep on keeping on at the things that really matter in their lives. We can see that their *time is rich*, and we sense our own lack in this regard. We want some of whatever medicine they're taking!

Well, it's not really a medicine, of course, but the prescription is available – free of charge – to FFs like me. I've learned (okay, I'm still learning) to take the medicine, and I want to encourage you to try it too.

All you need to do is to learn the key secret perspectives of CFs, in the two dimensions of **time** and **space**.

It's no more complicated than this: *My Time is Yours*, and *Front to Back*!

If you put these principles into practice, you'll soon find that the pursuit of perfection isn't a burden, far less a "waste" of time, but rather a gateway to truly *rich* time.

Idealists rather than realists

The CF mindset is free-spirited, tuned to the ethereal, the invisible, and the intangible.

Perhaps as a consequence of this natural tuning, many CFs are inclined to attempt those things that others (most likely FFs) consider to be *impractical* or even *impossible*.

The CF mindset is boundlessly enthusiastic and creative, pushing forward by means of trial-and-error into uncharted territories. CFs are authentic and passionate, relentlessly giving themselves in the service of something "bigger" – be that a close relationship, cause, or creed.

CFs don't put much stock in **systems**, whether creating these for their own use, or adopting those built by others. The great advantage of this is that it gives them high levels of *flexibility*.

If a CF *believes* in an interface, that interface can become all-consuming. When CFs get hold of a powerful message (or, better, when a powerful message gets hold of a CF – that's the usual pattern) they will devote themselves to the pursuit of its ideals, often persuading others to join them.

First Lady Eleanor Roosevelt was a shy and quiet girl, afraid of conflict and extremely sensitive to the expectations of others. (These last two are quite common CF traits, given the CF tendency to derive values from *outside* themselves.) But in later life, when thrust into the spotlight, she became an advocate for causes close to her heart. These included the labour conditions of the working classes and servicemen's charities. Much to her own surprise, and in ways that often belied her introversion, Eleanor became a front-line political activist.

Eleanor Roosevelt displayed classic CF characteristics, and she made excellent use of them for the good of society. She acted on the basis of her ideals, giving herself wholeheartedly to all-consuming causes that took her attention and concern. Like Queen Esther, she was catapulted into the public eye against all her expectations. But her openness to serendipity led her to the people and the principles that would shape both her life and the lives of countless others she affected.

CFs will aim high – often higher than internal and external constraints seem to permit. Sometimes, they won't make the mark, or hit the level they aim at. But for most CFs, that's not as disastrous as it might seem. CFs are relatively well-adjusted to the prospect of "failure." They would rather aim high (as high as they know) and fail to finish, than aim low and settle for what they see as mediocrity or compromise.

A mindset of wholehearted commitment to people and causes is a powerful one indeed. Harnessed in the right way, turned to the right interfaces, it truly has the power to change the world. But, on an individual, microcosmic level, CF idealism is a fruit of – and a catalyst for – rich time. There's a positive feedback loop here, as there is for all these positive characteristics we're thinking about. *Idealism* breeds *rich time* which breed more *idealism*.

But what if you're a natural FF? What if you are much more inclined to calculate and strategize, to determine the dimensions of time and space within which you're prepared to engage, before you begin? Is it possible to develop something of the idealism that characterises the CF mindset?

It certainly is! What you need to do is return to the key secret CF perspectives.

First, *My Time is Yours*: you need to **begin** by *committing* yourself to the interface, by acknowledging its *inherent* worth, and letting go of your tendency to foreclose engagement. It's about consciously taking your focus *off* the end-game (which is only in your own mind, anyway), and giving your attention to the here-and-now.

Second, *Front to Back*: some interfaces are simply unknown territory. The wise explorer in a new environment treads slowly and carefully, making sure not to jump the gun. *You can't make a map of a land you've never visited.* So, let the lie of the land make itself evident to you, step by humble step.

How long will that take? I can't tell you, and it's the wrong question to ask! Strive to maintain openness, and you'll find serendipity won't be far away.

Innovative rather than conventional

In Yoko Ogawa's prize-winning novel, *The Housekeeper and the Professor*, one of the main characters (known as "the professor") has a short-term memory span of just 80 minutes, as a result of a car accident. Each day, he has to start again with all his interfaces. For everyone else in the novel, it's like *Groundhog Day* every morning, because so many basics have to be repeated. And yet the professor's creativity seems to know no bounds, as he turns his attention to unsolved mathematical problems.

The CF mindset is able to operate in remarkably innovative ways. It is typically not bound by previous experience. In this sense, it is not encumbered with a constricting short-term memory span to hold it back. "Success" is a spur – not to press the *repeat* button, but to seek further new horizons. "Failure" simply renews the CF mindset's desire to get things "right" next time. Similarly, CFs are not bound by the "givens" that others may try to put upon them. They are free-thinking and creative, always searching for new approaches to their tasks, goals, and relationships.

In one sense, CFs never "arrive" at their destinations. This is what makes them so relentlessly innovative. CFs are *pioneers* rather than *settlers*, and *prospectors* rather than *residents*. Like the Johnny Appleseed of American legend, CFs are wandering souls, whose wandering makes sense to them in the context of the bigger picture, as they keep on the move to serve others and their ideals.

One great strength of the CF mindset is this willingness to try new things rather than get stuck. We've seen already that this can be a powerful gift in relationships. When the same old arguments seem to come up, or the same old problems surface, CFs are often able to think outside the box to look for material and emotional solutions.

CF innovation can lead directly to serendipitous discoveries. As you now know, I'm not a natural CF. But I'll share a recent example from my own experience, to show you that even default FFs can share in this innovative mindset, and open up new vistas in the process.

A few months ago, I was surfing the web and I found a list of online writing competitions. I'd tried a writing competition in my own (academic) subject – theology – once before, and I started thinking about having another go. Quite by chance, I found a competition that required essays on the subject of tackling climate change. Now, I knew *next to nothing* about climate change. I'd not studied science since school, and the extent of my knowledge on the subject was what I'd read in the newspapers – no more.

But I couldn't deny that the site sparked an interest. *Serendipity in action.* Over the next eight weeks, I spent many hours of my free time looking through library books and online articles about climate change. My mindset in respect of this interface was *My Time is Yours.*

Without any idea of where my essay might go (I didn't know enough about the subject to have an idea) I *had to* use the *Content-First* mindset. The project was open-ended. I didn't really know at first whether I would ever actually *start* writing the essay itself, let alone *finish* it. I was working from a *Front to Back* perspective, unnatural to me, but consciously adopted on this occasion.

Then one day after church I met someone for the first time and we got chatting over coffee. It turned out he was a scientist, working on carbon storage and capture (CSC) solutions to tackle climate change. Until I'd started my personal research, I'd never even *heard* of CSC. For the first time, I had a conversation with a climate change expert, about *his* specialist area, and I didn't feel like a complete fool! It was a great feeling.

Once I had an idea of what I wanted to write, my default FF mindset switched into gear. I decided time and space parameters, and the 20-page essay was written in super-quick time. Who knows if I'll win the competition. That's not the point. The point is the serendipity. I was open to something new, and something new came along. I learned a lot about something that was fresh to me, and important for the planet. It's sparked so many interesting conversations – with my kids, with my wife, and with friends.

And for me, it was an *out-of-my-comfort-zone* innovation.

Natural FF mindset readers may want to pause here to think about how they might innovate some more, by adopting the secret key perspectives of the CF mindset. Will it be in your relationships? In your work life? Or in an openness to a new interest, hobby, or field of learning.

Once again, the psychological keys are the two perspectives: *My Time is Yours*, and *Front to Back*. Once again, *rich* time awaits!

Spontaneous rather than strategic

CFs are gifted gear-shifters. They can adopt and adapt to new data easily, changing course multiple times without the anxiety that is commonly felt by default FFs. This makes CFs open to spontaneous decisions.

Spontaneity allows CFs to *take advantage of opportunities others might miss*. Operating according to a CF mindset, it's possible to make on-the-spot choices in response to new openings.

Spontaneity allows CFs to *miss dangers others might fall prey to*. When the CF mindset is engaged, a "set" course is not necessarily fixed, and the final destination is often unclear until the final moment. Had the captain of the *Titanic* been a natural CF, history might well have been very different!

On a day-to-day level, CFs will typically be more open to interruptions, corrections, advice, seemingly irrelevant "chatter," and various distractions – any of which may well open up serendipitous discoveries along the way.

In the theology faculty at Edinburgh University, where I've done my PhD study, there are three study rooms for postgraduate students. Each room seats about 12-20 students, and they're typically used as office bases for the three or four years of a PhD. The only marked difference between the rooms is the "culture." One of the rooms has a "silence" culture. The carrels (study booths) have high walls. The unwritten rule is that you can't talk inside the room. If someone's working in here, they're not to be disturbed. Some people even get twitchy about buzzing phones!

Another room has an "open discussion" culture. People do work in here too, but there's a much more relaxed atmosphere. The carrels don't have high walls. You can start a conversation with someone else – even across the room – and others may well join in. There's a good bit of office "banter." People will bounce ideas off others, and share their joys and frustrations with their research, or even just what they've seen on *Facebook* or *eBay*. This room is the original "chatroom"!

The third room aims at a middle way. You're allowed to talk to others, but you've got to keep your voice down a bit. If it's not a "work" conversation, you probably ought to take it outside. The walls between the carrels are at a kind of "middling" height – short enough to see over, but tall enough to hide behind if you want to keep your head down!

Where would you want to work?

My carrel was in this third room. I chose it in order to strike what I hoped would be a balance between *smart* working and *serendipitous* interactions. In retrospect, it wasn't ideal. On the basis of the principles I've shared in this book, what do you think would have been best? Right! It would have been better to spend about half my time in the "silent" room, and the other half in the "chatty" room. That should, in theory at least, have offered the best of both worlds, rather than a fudge between two, potentially powerful, poles.

Both strategy *and* spontaneity have their place in our interfaces, and CFs are typically rich in the latter. If you're an FF, and I've convinced you that it's worthwhile learning a CF mindset to complement your own natural strengths, you can work on developing the perspectives *My Time is Yours* and *Front to Back*. Or, you can think carefully about where to put your desk!

Weaknesses of the CF mindset

Let's pause for a brief summary. In this chapter I've taken us on a guided tour of the *Content-First* (FF) mindset, one of the two basic mindsets with which we human beings operate when we engage with the world.

Some readers will have CF as their natural default mindset. If that's you, this chapter will have felt like playing a home fixture: familiar and well-supported. You have a gift, for sure!

The CF mindset is *powerful*, and *essential* if we are to master our interfaces on the way to *time-rich living*. CFs typically find themselves encountering richness at every level of their lives.

The CF mindset is the foundation of the "serendipity" that makes *smart serendipity* the model for the time-rich life.

But the CF mindset by itself is insufficient. It's only one half of the whole. Remember, there are **two** basic mindsets, and without adopting **both** of them, we will never be truly time-rich.

Indeed, there are certain interfaces for which the CF mindset is obviously not a natural fit. These include the following:

· *Decision-making*

The CF mindset thrives on *openness*, and so it can have a hard time with *closing down* on something. FOMO (*Fear of Missing Out*) may be a factor here, but at least as significant is the typical CF struggle to see the end from the beginning. Without a clear view of where a decision may lead, it's hard to make that decision. Interfaces that demand defined dimensions, such as individual work assignments, are a CF weakness because they require up-front decision making in the dimensions of time and space.

· Hard conversations

CFs are often reluctant to engage complex issues or conflicts face-on, but prefer to dodge difficult issues by changing tack or trying a new approach. This can be a strength if a problem is resolvable by creativity, but it is a weakness if longstanding and intractable issues need attention. CF bosses can cause their staff considerable frustration by appearing unwilling to tackle hard issues in the workplace.

· Deadlines

This is perhaps the CF weakness that is most obvious to observers. CFs are *last-minute people*. As we've seen, this is because they put *content* over *form*, choosing not to "boss" their interfaces, but rather allowing their interfaces to "boss" them. The *interface* (not the *individual*) determines the time and energy that will be spent, and so CFs will keep on going at their interfaces until they are forced to stop by an outside boundary such as deadline imposed by a boss or client.

· Sealing a deal

Once again, the flipside of openness to opportunity is a failure to effect closure. CFs may see many more chances come floating down the river, but they will let many of them float away, through lack of time, organisation, and structure.

· Turning dreams into reality

CFs are big on dreams. A CFs bucket-list will probably be longer and more varied than an FF's. It will probably include ideas and ideals that aim for the stars. CFs are full of ideas, and constantly find new ones coming to them, both from within and from without. But often, the CF mindset is ill-suited to converting these dreams into reality. The dreams remain poorly-defined and few strategic plans are put in place to realise them.

Because of their tendency to prioritise *surfing* over *searching*, CFs often have a tough time when it comes to interfaces that demand a *form-first* approach. And so their lives are characterised by a lack of smartness: *the unfortunate truth is that they fail to make good on so much promise!*

CFs are the people who are always short of time. They let their interfaces "boss" them, and so they tend to lose control. That's why CFs who haven't developed the FF mindset as a second operating mindset for certain interfaces are *not truly time-rich.*

If you're an CF by nature, and you've read this far, I hope you can see that your default mindset isn't always optimal. There are some significant weaknesses to it. That's why you need to cultivate the FF mindset as well. You might want to look back at chapter two, or read that chapter for the first time if you started with this one.

If you have a natural FF preference, I'm pretty sure you'll have found this chapter a challenge at times. As I said at the beginning, I'm an FF, and I found this chapter much harder to write! But I have made some progress in adopting CF as a second mindset, and so I hope you can be encouraged that it's not too difficult to learn. Now that you know the two key secret perspectives of the CF mindset, you can begin to apply them to your interfaces.

In the last chapter, we need to tackle the outstanding elephant in the room: *which mindset do we use when?* It's all very well knowing about – or even possessing – the perspectives that make up both mindsets, but we need to know when and how to switch between them.

I have both "plus" and "minus" screwdrivers in my toolkit. I know which one to use depending on the type of screw-head. In the same way, the type of interface determines the mindset we need to apply at any given time. Let me explain…

4 WHICH MINDSET WHEN?

"Seeing reality for what it is, is what we call discernment.
The work of discernment is very hard."
· Lewis B. Smedes

"You'd be surprised how many people violate this simple principle every day of their
lives and try to fit square pegs into round holes, ignoring the clear reality that
Things Are As They Are."
· Benjamin Hoff

We've covered a lot of ground in the previous three chapters.

I'm going to assume that, by now, you know whether you naturally default to a *Form-First* or a *Content-First* mindset. I'm also going to assume that you now have a good idea of your own strengths and weaknesses when you apply your default mindset to your interfaces. Finally, I'm going to assume that you have at least the *desire* to learn and develop the mindset that is the polar-opposite of your natural preference, in order to foster *smart serendipity* in your interfaces, and experience more *time-rich living*.

It's worth reminding ourselves that FF and CF really are *polar opposites*. People who attempt a one-size-fits-all approach to their interfaces, trying to find some kind of happy middle way between the poles, are likely to be disappointed. Neither hot nor cold, their approach is best characterised as "lukewarm," and while it may avoid the worst excesses of either pole gone wrong, I believe it is almost *never* the optimal mindset.

Everything we do is best approach according to *either* an FF *or* a CF mindset.

Already in this book, I've provided you with a "toolkit" to help you to understand and employ both mindsets. We've also looked at a whole range of specific and concrete situations when either an FF or a CF approach might be optimal. I hope many readers will have begun to use some of these tools already, particularly the new ones!

In this final chapter, we're going to zoom back out and do some big-picture thinking about *which* mindset we need to adopt *when*. I hope this will give you a whole-of-life view of the value of thinking about your interfaces in this way. And I hope it will also provide a key to the discernment question that – ultimately – unlocks the door to *smart serendipity*.

Clearing away some misunderstandings

Having read this far, some readers might draw the mistaken conclusion that what I'm advocating in this book is basically a healthy "work-life balance."

Now, I think that *time-rich living* may well lead indirectly to something like a good work-life balance, but the conclusion that that's what this book is all about would be wrong, for two reasons.

First, although an FF mindset might well be particularly useful for many people, in most of their interfaces, in a majority of workplaces, that does *not* mean that FF is the "work" mindset, and "CF" is the "life" mindset.

For one thing, there are many different types of work. Work that is primarily creative, for example, is not likely to be best-suited to an FF mindset. Also, even in an office job, there will be particular interfaces that require a CF mindset. We won't always be best-served by turning on an FF mindset at work and a CF mindset at home.

Second, talk of a "work-life balance" tends to put the focus on two things we "do" – *work* and *life*, so that we can work out a better "balance" between them. But the FF and CF mindsets are not, themselves, *things we do*! They are approaches to our interfaces!

Another mistaken conclusion would be that the FF mindset works best when the object of our interface is *inanimate*, and the CF mindset works best when the object is *animate*.

In simpler language, FF is for *things*, and CF is for *people*.

As a general rule, there is probably some truth in this. There's not a lot to be gained through having an open-ended, idealistic interaction with a stapler!

But it certainly doesn't hold true all the time. For example, we've seen that bringing the CF mindset to a library (full of *things*) can open a world of possibilities. And few interfaces can be more frustrating than a weekly team meeting (full of *people*) run on CF principles.

In this book, *smartness* and *serendipity* are distinguished – and come together again – in a distinctive way, that's not as simple as the *work-life*, or *things-people* dualities might suggest. Let me explain.

The Make-Time / Take-Time paradigm

I can distil the main message of this chapter into just four short sentences:

> **Smart interfaces** *make time.*
> **Serendipitous interfaces** *take time.*
>
> **Smart interfaces** *make space.*
> **Serendipitous interfaces** *take space.*

This is the key to discerning which mindset to adopt for any given interface, and therefore the key to experiencing *time-rich living*!

Here's how it works.

When you use the FF mindset, your aim should be to **make** *time and space.*

This is the ultimate potential of the FF mindset.

Remember the first key secret perspective of the FF mindset: *Time is Mine.* FFs "boss" their interfaces, determining in advance how much time to spend on them. They make that determination, *not* according to the supposed "value" of the interface, but by the amount of time they have available – ultimately, the amount of time they *want* to spend on the interface.

And don't forget the second key secret perspective of the FF mindset: *Back to Front*. FFs start any interface with an end-game in view, and calculate from there how to engineer the interface in order to arrive at the desired result. They *first* "create" space (conceptually or concretely) and *then* they fill it up.

Working according to these two key secret perspectives in the dimensions of time and space, FFs are the masters of their time. They are *strategic*: planning in advance and setting parameters before beginning. They are *conventional*: developing and perfecting processes and systems to streamline success. They are *realist*: working in the real world with sensitivity to constraints and limitations. And they are *finishers*: perhaps above all, the FF mindset *gets things done, quickly and well*.

This is why the FF mindset – at its best – can *make time and space*.

So, when is the FF mindset optimal? What interfaces demand it?

The answer is simple. The FF mindset should be used when you want to *make time and space*. When you want to *finish* an interface, strategically, realistically, according to tried-and-tested means – in order to *make time and space for something or someone else*.

It should be obvious that such an interface might have an inanimate object. If I have a job to do at work, I may want to finish it in a timely and effective manner, *so that I can get on with something else*. I should apply the FF mindset, and get determining time and space parameters without delay.

But equally, such an interface may well have an animate object. I may be engaged in a conversation or a meeting with someone from whom I need a certain favour, and it may be my priority to sort that out as quickly and efficiently as possible, *because there are other tasks that are also pressing upon me*. The optimal way to proceed is to adopt the FF mindset, and put my end-game in place so that I am clear about my objectives.

The key point is that the FF mindset *makes time and space*. Now, of course it doesn't make time and space *absolutely*. We're all finite. We all have our allotted times and places. There are only twenty-four hours in the day. If time and space were limitless, the world would be the CF's oyster. It's because they are *not* that we need the FF mindset too. It makes time and space *relatively*. By enabling the efficient, *smart* completion of interfaces, the

FF mindset makes time and space for us to do other things.

But what are these "other things"? That's where the CF mindset comes in!

When you use the CF mindset, your aim should be to **take** *time and space*.

That is the ultimate potential of the CF mindset.

Remember the first key secret perspective of the CF mindset: *My Time is Yours*. CFs determine how much time and energy to spend on any particular interface by the "value" they attach to that interface, and they find the value *in* the interface. Things are valuable, in the CF mindset, because of the value they inherently possess, and it's our job to approach them in such a way that corresponds to their value.

And then, there's the second key secret perspective of the CF mindset: *Front to Back*. CFs start with where they are, and move forward incrementally, with a high level of openness to changing direction or even finishing without a resolution of any sort, if circumstances demand it. CFs *first* experience *content*, and only *then* do they think about applying a *form* to it.

These two perspectives help make CFs incredibly open to *rich* experience. They are *perfectionists*: they take their time, they work with what they've got, and they don't give up on it – thorough, and thoroughly committed. They're *idealists*: free-spirited, tuned to the ethereal, the invisible, and the intangible, boundlessly enthusiastic and creative, authentic and passionate, relentlessly giving themselves in the service of something "bigger" – be that a close relationship, cause, or creed. They're *innovative*: free-thinking and creative, always searching for new approaches to their tasks, goals, and relationships. And they're *spontaneous*: ready to take advantage of opportunities, and open to the distractions which open them up to serendipity.

This is why the CF mindset – at its best – can *take time and space*.

So, when should you seek to engage your interfaces with the CF mindset? The answer is that it is optimal for any situation when you want to *take time and space*. When you sense that an interface needs to be open-ended, because it's either (a) too important, or (b) too pregnant with opportunity for *you* to set the parameters of engagement – *that's* when you need the CF approach.

Of course, the most obvious example of this might be your closest relationships. The CF mindset is well-suited for your relationships with your partner and family. It is likely also to be the best approach for your relationships with friends and perhaps even co-workers. If you naturally prefer the FF mindset, you'll need to keep working at this one, especially when your relationships go through rocky patches. Serendipity in relationships is one of the most exciting things we can experience. It might mean that we meet someone for the first time. Or it may mean we keep on discovering new things about – or together with – a life-partner, even after many years of being together.

Another example of when the CF mindset is most appropriate is in pursuing the big questions of life: meaning, identity, and destiny. Or the great values: truth, goodness, and beauty. Almost by definition, we can't set the parameters for these questions. At its most responsible, natural science recognises its limitations here, and so should we. Serendipity in the spiritual begins with the willingness to admit our ignorance, or at least that we might be wrong. It doesn't necessarily mean that we are always and forever "seekers." We should seek to *find*. Some readers may have found what they are looking for already. But we would be wise not to decide in advance what we are looking for.

Remember: serendipity is not just about me, or you. Something – or someone – may well find us!

So, if you want to *make* time and space, you need to think *Form-First*. If you want to *take* time and space, you need to think *Content-First*. That's the basic paradigm for discernment.

It sounds simple, and it really is. But so many people make the wrong decisions about what mindset to apply to which interfaces. That might be because they haven't learned how to operate except according to their natural default type. Or, it might be because they haven't worked out their own priorities and applied the appropriate mindsets accordingly.

Let's see what that might look like in practice.

Mapping your own priorities

To enjoy *time-rich living*, it's important that – as far as possible – you decide what interfaces will be *time and space-making* (because you will "boss" them with an FF mindset, to complete them as efficiently and effectively as

71

possible) and what interfaces will be *time-taking* (because you will allow them to "boss" you with a CF mindset, determining their own time and space according to their intrinsic values).

A helpful way to begin (or to crystallise) the discernment process is to make a list.

Your first list should be all the interfaces (tasks, relationships *etc.*) that are either *currently* part of your life, or else those that you would *like* to be part of your life.

You might come up with a list along these lines:

o Dinner with friends
o Work report
o Visiting the library
o Long-term project at work
o Networking evening
o Thinking about big questions
o Writing a book
o Helping at the soup kitchen
o Focusing on retirement plans
o Language study
o Tax return
o Planning next year's holiday with the kids
o Email admin
o Travelling
o Visiting client
o After-work drinks
o Talking to colleague about next year's budget
o Walking in the woods
o Team meeting

Of course, your list will be different from mine – which is only an example anyway.

Next, you want to divide these interfaces in *two* lists, in accordance with the *Make-Time / Take-Time* paradigm. This is where you need to think hard, and apply some of the knowledge you've gained from this book, as well as your own personal preferences and goals.

Your lists might look something like this:

· *Making* **time and space** (Remember, it's not that *you* make time and space *for* these interfaces, it's that these interfaces "make" time and space for you because of the way you approach them.)

- o Work report
- o Tax return
- o Team meeting
- o Email admin
- o Language study
- o Visiting client
- o After-work drinks
- o Talking to colleague about next year's budget

· *Taking* **time and space** (Remember, these are the interfaces that, because of their intrinsic value, you want to approach as open-ended, serendipitous experiences.)

- o Visiting the library
- o Planning next year's holiday with the kids
- o Long-term project at work
- o Walking in the woods
- o Helping at the soup kitchen
- o Networking evening
- o Dinner with friends
- o Thinking about big questions
- o Writing a book
- o Travelling
- o Focusing on retirement plans

The first thing I want to stress about these lists is that they're just examples. Depending on your circumstances and judgment, "planning next year's holiday with the kids" could well be a time-*making* interface that you could finish off in 10 minutes, saving lots of fighting and hundreds of pounds in the process! Equally, "language study" might well be, for you, an activity to approach serendipitously. You may not even know what language you're going to study yet!

The second thing to note is that the lists don't necessarily reflect an order of importance. Completing your tax return isn't *less* important than a long-term work project. You've got to do both. And so what you're discerning here is the *kind* of approach that you're going to take to each interface.

You *could* complete your tax return according to a CF mindset. Plenty of people do. (I know this, because I've been a tax accountant!) They file right on the deadline, or late. They take *ages* sorting out spreadsheets and never really getting round to finishing off.

Or you could do it according to an FF mindset – quickly, efficiently, accurately – to make time and space for other things.

What making lists like these does help with is giving you a picture of what your *time-rich life* might look like. It's great motivation!

One other self-diagnostic you can perform with these lists is to ask yourself: *where do I struggle to apply the optimal mindset?* For example, you may find it relatively easy to think *My Time is Yours* when you're volunteering at the soup kitchen, but less so when your partner wants to talk to you about something, or just to hang out together.

These points of potential "mismatch" between (on the one hand) the optimal mindset for an interface and (on the other hand) your natural preference will be – I hope – the greatest areas for growth and development for you as a result of reading this book. If you're a natural CF, that may involve a smarter approach to some of your interfaces. If your instinctive preference is for FF, that may involve a new openness to serendipity in your life.

Giving time and space

Being selfish is bad for us. That principle applies to what we do with our money. It also applies to what we do with our time and space.

Scientific research supports these assertions.[5] What psychologists call "prosocial behaviour" is proven to be healthy for us. Giving our time and space to *other people* (and to a lesser but still significant extent, *other causes*) – in all kinds of ways – increases our feeling of "time affluence." In other words, it's a way to enjoy *time-rich living.*

This is such an important point that it needs a little section of this book all to itself! The first key secret perspective of the FF mindset is *Time is Mine.* If you take it at face value, it sounds selfish. But it mustn't be a self-serving end.

Please don't think that the pursuit of *time-rich living* is meant to be self-centred! It *could* be that, of course. But it *needn't* be. It's what you make of it.

My *Time is Mine*, only so that I have time to give to others, and so: *My Time is Yours*.

I need the FF mindset to boss *some* of my interfaces, precisely so that I have the time and space to give to others. With the FF mindset, I can *make* time. But that time is time to be *taken* doing something else – something else that matters deeply to me.

Our time and space are not like our money. Money is – at least in theory – a resource that we can grow and grow indefinitely, or else lose completely. Time is not like that. We have 24 hours in each day. That's the same as every other person on the planet. We can't have any more. And we can't have any less, either.

The question is not, therefore, how can we make *more* time. It's how can we make the *richest* time. And one way we do that is – perhaps counter-intuitively – by ensuring that we give our time away.

It's the same with our space. We all occupy a certain place at any given time, and we can't be in two places at once. When we try to – like when our minds drift away from where we are and from the people around us – we're usually not very effective. We can't make *more* space.

So again, the question is how best to use the space we've got. Giving it to others (others we care about, who are engaged in causes that are important to us, or just others less fortunate than ourselves in some way) is one way to use our space well. It's good for others. And it's good for us.

Serendipity that's *smart*

It's time to draw this book to a close.

I want to thank you – the reader – for reading this book. You're a busy person – I'm guessing – and there are plenty of other books out there. *But you read this one*. I'm deeply grateful.

Was that a strategic choice on your part? Were you *searching* for something – perhaps some straight talking and practical suggestions to help you negotiate the challenges of a busy life?

Or was this a serendipitous discovery? Were you *surfing* – and you came upon this book and decided to give it a try?

Whichever it was, I hope you've found it time well spent. It's been a lot of fun to write.

I hope you've learned more about yourself, and your strengths and weaknesses.

I hope you've got a better idea of why you tend to approach the interfaces in your life in particular ways.

I hope you've been excited by the challenges and possibilities of doing things differently.

I hope you now know what aspects of your mindset you'd like to work on and develop.

I hope you're ready to enjoy a life of *smart serendipity*!

In one sense, *we all know what tomorrow holds*. Just look at your diary. It may well be full. Multiple *known interfaces* await you. Some you have chosen. Others have chosen you. But here's one thing you always control: *It's entirely up to you what mindset you bring to them.*

In another sense, *none of us know what tomorrow holds*, for good or for ill. There are so many *unknowns* in our lives. Are you ready to take advantage of the surprises? With the right mindset, you can be open to the good things you might never otherwise have known.

May you enjoy true time richness – and the truly richest of times!

AFTERWORD

CAN A PASTOR REALLY WRITE SELF-HELP BOOKS?

The short answer to this question is *yes*. I'm a pastor (at least, I *was*) and you're now reading my book!

But there's a bit more to say, by way of an afterword to this book. This is more of a personal reflection, as well as a parting thought to leave with you.

So-called "self-help" books have a bit of a bad rap among pastors. I have, myself, counselled people to steer clear of the self-help section in bookshops, if what they're looking for is *real truths* about life, the universe, and everything – or just about why we're here and what it's all about.

As a Christian pastor, it's my job to direct people to *the Bible* for truths like these. That's where I believe they'll find answers to life's fundamental questions.

Some "self-help" books, perhaps based on particular spiritualities or philosophies, will suggest that you can get answers to life's big questions from looking within yourself, and drawing on your own resources. For the authors of these books, it really is all about *self*-help.

I can't go along with that, I'm afraid. I agree that it's important to *know yourself*. I've written about that in this book. But I *don't* think all knowledge, wisdom, inspiration, and truth comes from within. Whether we *search*, or *surf,* we need to look *outside ourselves.*

Our "help" has to come from somewhere else.

I can write a book like this because I believe that God has made human beings with great potential, and there are wonderful things we can all do if and when we put our minds to it. We can all share wisdom and learn from one another. Theologians call this *common grace.*

But there's also something called *special grace.*

Finding God in Jesus Christ has been the ultimate serendipity in my life: *the most valuable, surprising discovery I've ever made.* In this case, my "smartness" had nothing to do with it. I was "found." That was God's *special grace.*

When Jesus Christ found me, I said to him, in effect, *My Time is Yours.* Each day he leads me to interfaces of all types, and shows me how to *make* time and space with some of them, so that I can *take* time and space for others. Life with Jesus is both *Front to Back* – one step at a time – and *Back to Front* – because the final destination is sure.

It seems to me that behind every "serendipity," someone (not me) has a smart plan.
So, *Seek, Search,* and *Surf… and you will find!*

REFERENCES

[1] "World is angry and stressed, Gallup report says," *BBC News*, 26 April 2019, https://www.bbc.co.uk/news/world-48063982, accessed 26 April 2019.

[2] "If you never have enough time… then slow down," *The Guardian*, 16 July 2017, https://www.theguardian.com/lifeandstyle/2017/jul/16/if-you-never-have-enough-time-then-slow-down, accessed 26 April 2019.

[3] I have a suspicion that FFs will instinctively prefer to begin with their weaknesses, and so many of them will skip to chapter 3 at this point. CFs will naturally incline towards not skipping anything, and so their preference will probably be to go straight on to chapter 2.

[4] This story is told in a Japanese book: Yoshinori Kawakita, *"Jibun no Jikan" no Tsukurikata・Tanoshimikata: Ikigai wo Mistukeru Hassojutsu* (Tokyo, PHP Publishing: 1997), Kindle, no. 195. I haven't been able to find the anecdote in any English sources.

[5] See the article from Stanford Business School at https://www.gsb.stanford.edu/insights/frank-flynn-giving-gift-time-others, accessed 6 May 2019.

ABOUT THE AUTHOR

Richard Brash was born in Edinburgh. He has worked as a school teacher, a tax accountant in the City of London, and a student pastor. He is currently a PhD student at the University of Edinburgh. He is married, with two children.

Printed in Poland
by Amazon Fulfillment
Poland Sp. z o.o., Wrocław